NATIONAL SERVICE HIGH JINKS

(a young man's story 1947-49)

Eric M. Malcolm

Published in 2018 by
Moira Brown
Broughty Ferry
Dundee. DD5 2HZ
www.publishkindlebooks4u.co.uk

National Service High Jinks was first published
as a kindle book in 2013.

ISBN13: 978 1 98305 950 6

FOREWARD

I was called up on Thursday, 5 June, 1947, exactly a month after my 18th birthday; under the National Service Acts of 1939-1946. No specific length of service was mentioned in these Acts, but, by the time I was called up, it was generally recognized that the period of service was two years. This was substantiated in December 1947, yet, for some obscure reason, I served two years, three weeks and two days.

After six weeks basic training with the Black Watch at Queens Barracks in Perth, I was sent to Barnard Castle in Yorkshire to train as a Tech. Ack. (Technical Assistant) in the Royal Artillery. For the remainder of my time, I was based at Milton Barracks in Gravesend with spells at Stiffkey, Lenton Hurst, Langham, Bostal Heath, Welbeck and Weybourne.

Following my demob (demobilization) on 27 June, 1949, I became what was known as a 'Z Man', i.e. on the reserve list. But, when I was recalled to the colours, illness prevented me from going.

As I have letters I wrote to my parents, plus diaries, I have been able to recount my exploits as if they occurred yesterday instead of over half a century ago. The direct speech is, of course, not exactly verbatim, but serves to illustrate what was said at the time.

I must acknowledge the encouragement and support given by my brother, Ian, who nagged me into putting my experiences down on paper and put the whole thing together on his word processor.

E.M.M.

PRIVATE 19179228, QUEEN'S BARRACKS, PERTH

On 24 March, 1947 I underwent a medical examination in Dundee's Caird Hall building to ascertain if I was fit for National Service. I believed that I was in first class condition, but, because I was slim for my height of 5' 11", the doctor said, "I think I'll make you Grade II, but you'll be Grade I in no time." After the medical, a Military Interviewing Officer asked which Service I would like to join, and, as I had no preference, it is likely that he wrote down Army. In any case, MIOs hadn't the power to implement a choice.

On Thursday 22 May, I received my call-up notice, instructing me to report between 9am and 12 noon, or as soon as possible thereafter, on Thursday, 5 June to No.42 General Service Corps at Queen's Barracks, Perth. And so, exactly one month after my 18th birthday, I entered the Barracks to begin basic training as a soldier of the King (George VI). The new entrants were formed into Squads 4, 5 on Thursday, 5 June and 6 and I was assigned to No.5.

Although we had all already been medically examined, we were examined again, inoculated against I don't know what, and our teeth inspected. We were each provided with a Service Book and Pay Book, and advised to tip the barber *before* we had our hair cut, as, otherwise, he was likely to be vicious! Neither sheets nor pyjamas was supplied and, although some slept the first night in the pyjamas they had brought, henceforth we slept in the vest and underpants we had worn during the day. On that first night, I found the pillow so brick hard that I had difficulty in sleeping.

Clothing was issued the following day and we had to stencil the last four digits of our service number on everything we received which included two battledresses (a 'best' and a 'second best') and a set of denims. Oddly enough, I was given a 'best' uniform unlike the others. It was a Canadian battledress and beret in light green, instead of khaki, and, because of this, visitors would stop and comment on my smart appearance during future inspections of the ranks.

We were issued with two pairs of boots and, as neither pair fitted me, a large blister formed on one of my heels. After a medical orderly lanced the blister with a razor and daubed the area with methylated spirits, I had to return immediately to the parade ground, but henceforth wore spongy soles in my boots. To provide a high shine on new boots, they required boning with a heated spoon to smooth the dimpled leather before the application of spit and polish.

On weekdays, reveille was at 6.30am, breakfast at 7am, dinner at 12.30pm and tea, the last meal of the day, at 4.30pm. On Sundays, reveille was at 7.45am, with breakfast at 8am. I had no complaints about the food and snacks could be had in the Church of Scotland canteen.

Although, on morning parade, we were ordered to shave daily, some recruits tried, unsuccessfully, to make a shave last for two days. Some with fair hair had virtually no visible growth, yet an NCO warned them that he didn't want to see that fluff tomorrow. Incidentally, tea was poured into our mugs from buckets and, as it tasted peculiar, it was rumoured that it contained bromide - a method reputed to be used by the Army to reduce the sex urge.

The large barrack room had deep wooden boxes, at the foot of our beds, instead of lockers. We were instructed how to make our beds for inspection and, when an NCO entered the room, the order was, 'STAND BY YOUR BED.' Laundry was uplifted once a week and, on one occasion, I was detailed with four others to iron the uniforms of our squad. Kit inspection was no mere formality as, with everything having to be neatly laid in a particular way, it seemed to involve an amazing amount of work. And as blancoing was an ongoing chore, we were instructed in how to do it.

Squad drill on the parade ground was a serious business and, for the first week or two, a cause of concern for the capable NCOs, as some recruits swung both arms in unison while one put his right arm forward with his right foot and his left arm forward with his left foot! To correct these faults, the NCOs marched with the culprits, holding their arms to their sides.

By the end of the second week, we all swung our arms shoulder high and, being almost six feet tall, I was made the right-hand marker. "You're marching towards a cliff," said the corporal, "The orders HALT, RIGHT TURN and LEFT TURN cannot be given so what order can stop you going over the cliff?" And, as silence greeted the question, he continued, "The order is TO THE FRONT SALUTE so let's learn that one now." (On this order, we halted, saluted, about turned and marched off - every action being, as always, to the count of three.)

Drilling with fixed bayonets was unpopular, as novices can be careless in handling the weapon to the detriment of a neighbour. We were also made to charge and stick the bayonet into a straw dummy and, when the instructor bawled, "IN. TWIST.", the more squeamish were reluctant to TWIST.   Instruction was given in dismantling, assembling and firing the Lee Enfield .303 rifle, Bren and Sten guns and in unpinning and throwing uncharged hand grenades. Then there was the gas chamber where, after a few minutes, we were ordered to remove our masks and exit without panicking.   Great competition was engendered between the squads and, on the rifle range, the proceeds of a 3d sweep were given to the man who won.

Wearing sports kit, we did a 1¾ miles run round the North Inch, but one good runner kept going and was never seen again! It was compulsory to go to the baths after the run and, when a swimming gala was held that evening, I came in third at the crawl.

To toughen us up, four of us were ordered to fight each other in a ring. No boxing skill was involved, but the survivor was deemed champion. Concerning toughness, I regarded my squad as nothing more or less than a fair cross section of society, but when my pal, Jimmy Wilson, entered the barracks a month later, he called them a bunch a ruffians and said he was glad he wasn't among them.

In order to instil a pride in the regiment, we had lectures on the history and battle honours of the Black Watch although we were in the General Service Corps and did not wear the red hackle in our caps as our instructors did. There was no restriction in going out in the evenings and I often went to the pictures with Tom Bamburgh who had worked beside me in the office of Thomas Bonar & Co. Ltd.   Apart from one weekend when No.5 was Duty Squad and I was detailed to clean the Sergeants' Mess and the Cookhouse, while others peeled spuds, etcetera, I was able to hitch hike home at weekends. A large mirror at the gate allowed us to inspect ourselves before we appeared in public.

One sunny afternoon, we were marched into the countryside carrying full pack. An unladen sergeant, corporal and lance corporal accompanied us and, as the sergeant was anxious to beat another squad back to barracks, he set a good pace. Unfortunately, he took a wrong turning and, when he increased the pace, it proved too much for many of the heavily laden recruits. And, with the object of beating the other squad in their minds, the NCOs. resorted to carrying the rifles of those in distress. My father had provided me with a leather money belt, but due to the summer heat, I soon discarded it.

The fact that the pre-Army doctor had pronounced me Grade II gave my superiors cause for concern so that they considered sending me somewhere to be fattened up. But, when they found that I was coping well with basic training, this was not mentioned again.

Although our NCOs were pleasant and decent blokes, respected by the men, an unknown lance corporal threatened to charge me with DUMB INSOLENCE because I looked him straight in the eye. "And get your heels together when I'm talking to you," he growled.

Our own lance corporal was an old soldier compared to the sergeant and corporal and, when he spoke to Tom and me about being short of cash to enable him to attend a dress-uniform dance, we helped him out. This turned out to our advantage as, not only did he pay back the money during the following week, but put our names forward to be collectors on a flag day. And, as the townspeople were pleasant and generous, we thoroughly enjoyed the experience.

We were all interviewed by the Personnel Selection Officer (PSO) who placed us into one of the Summed Selection Groups (graded 1 to 5) according to his assessment; with other factors such as educational standard, intelligence test and basic training performance taken into consideration.

When the bell sounded in the small room in which I waited, I stepped out into the corridor to find it contained so many doors that I had difficulty in selecting the one to enter. "Where the dickens have you been?" asked the PSO.
To which I replied, "If your door was marked PSO, sir, I would have found it more easily."

After telling me to sit down, the PSO said, "What would you like to be in the Army?" And, when I replied, "I'd like to be an officer," he became friendly and explained that his job was to post men to various regiments and that I should apply for a commission after posting. "How would a course involving calculations suit you?" he asked. "Yes," I replied.
But when he went on to speak of geometry and trigonometry, I said, "I have little knowledge of these."
"But you can learn," he said. I thanked him and left, no doubt succeeded by another interviewee searching for his room.

I was right-hand marker of the squad, in line for a coveted green lanyard. But Sgt. Smith was not happy with our marching and eventually reached the conclusion that it was my fault. "You are one quarter pace out," he explained.   I was moved to position 3 in the front rank and Tom became marker and won the prize. When he sympathized with me for losing the honour, I said, "Forget it, Tom, I don't want to be so expert at marching and rifle drill that I'm posted to an infantry regiment." And this unexpected reply caused him concern for some time.

But the PSO must have placed me in a reasonably high SSG, as I was the only one posted to Deerbolt Camp to train as a Technical Assistant (Tech. Ack.) in the 38th Training Regiment of the Royal Artillery. And Tom went into the Royal Army Ordnance Corps, at Hillsea Barracks in Portsmouth. Passing-out parades were held every fortnight and, on Monday, 14 July, I enjoyed marching through Perth to the strains of the Black Watch Pipe Band.

DEERBOLT CAMP, BARNARD CASTLE, YORKSHIRE

Deerbolt Camp occupied an ideal site; to the west of Barnard Castle and on the opposite side of the River Tees from the ruined 12th century castle where Richard III once stayed. The period of training to become a Tech. Ack. was 4 months and the training regiment was composed of two signals' batteries and one Tech. Ack. battery. The latter was 193 Battery and I was placed in quad 70A. On my first morning at the Camp, we were awakened by the sound of a bugle, but no-one rose until bawled out of bed.

To my knowledge, Deerbolt was the only place in the U.K. where the mathematics of field gunnery was taught. Many of the intake had the benefit of higher education, but some, like me, had left school at 15 and all, including a bookie's runner and a bricklayer, had an aptitude for mathematics. The intake was billeted in two huts, grouped into A and B squads, and the first days were spent settling in. There were metal lockers beside each bed, a stove in the middle of each hut, a table and chairs. On the first Wednesday, and typical of the Army, we polished the floor, scrubbed the table and dusted everywhere for a billet inspection which did not materialize. We were, however, allowed more freedom than I had experienced during basic training in Perth although this was somewhat restricted by our gunnery instructor, Sergeant Sharples.

SERGEANT SHARPLES

Sharples set out to instil fear into us and in this he was successful. At Oswestry in Shropshire, the gunners' course lasted eight weeks, but Sharples' job was to convert us into competent gunners in only four. Two gunners were made to run round and round the gun park because they had moved instead of coming to attention and another two were made to hold two 25-pound shells above their heads because they yawned. And when their faces became ashen, Sharples bawled, "Don't faint. Don't dare faint." No one was allowed to walk on the gun park. It was always 'at the double'.

Inspecting us in the ranks one day, Sharples spotted a gunner with a dirty neck. Addressing two others, he shouted, "Take him away and give him a bath."
"School Certificate?" was his favourite question and "Yes, sergeant," was the usual reply.
"Yet you can't even tie your boot laces." And we didn't dare laugh.

But there was an occasion when the question brought a negative reply so that Sharples expressed surprise and asked, "Then what are you doing here among all those bright boys?" The gunner's response, however, proved to be like giving an apple to a teacher and, from then on, he was the sergeant's favourite.

One sunny afternoon, Sharples was in either a bad or a mad mood as he ordered us to put the guns into action, touch a distant tree and put the guns out of action – all at the double. "Sergeant," said one of the gunners.
"Yes?" queried Sharples.
"That tree is on the other side of the river."
"So what?" asked Sharples.
"But," explained the gunner, "I can't swim."
"Then you'll drown, won't you?" was the unsympathetic reply.
"Sergeant," I said.
"Now what?" he asked.
"I'm wearing my best boots because my others are in for repair."
And the response to that was, "That's your worry."

We jumped over a parapet and scrambled down the slope into the flowing river. Fortunately, it was deep only in the middle and those who could swim helped the others across. After touching the specified tree, we plunged back into the river and charged back to put the guns out of action. But the episode had not been without casualties. One gunner had an injured arm while another had fallen into nettles and, as we were without shirts and wearing shorts, he was badly stung. After blaming them for their carelessness, Sharples allowed them to go to the MI room. On another occasion, when Sharples considered three men had dirty necks, he made them wash in the river.

One day, singling out the gun crew I was in, Sharples remarked, "It's rather strange. You lot are always the slowest into action, yet the fastest out of action. How do you explain that?" We didn't – at least, not to him.

Towards the end of the gunnery course, we drove, with eight 25-pounder guns, to a driving range. Live shells were issued, the sequence of fire discipline observed and, after the guns were fired individually, there was an interval. All went well until the procedure was repeated. A cartridge case which hadn't been properly placed in the breach, fell out; just missing the iron platform. Sgt. Sharples took over and, on releasing the unfired shell, handed it to the crew's No.1 with the instruction to lay it very carefully on the ground some hundred yards away. Quite obviously, there was an element of risk involved and, as the No.1 was the gunner without his school certificate and Sharples favourite, we were surprised that he was chosen for the task.

About three weeks after completing the gunner course, the squad was performing gunnery drill under the supervision of 2nd Lieut. Smith, from Broughty Ferry. And, considering that we were sloppy, he marched us into the care of Sergeant Sharples to whom, as a perfectionist, this was an insult. But although it was he who then made us sweat by ordering us to run about while holding 25-pound shells above our heads, our anger was directed at Smith and not at him. I consoled my fellow squaddies by saying that I would *get* Smith when demobbed, but, of course, I never did and, on the sole occasion I saw Smith, I ignored him.

CHURCH PARADES

The regiment assembled on the square for church parades; held at 11am on weekdays when padres of various denominations came to the camp. Roman Catholics formed a large group, Protestants, Methodists and Baptists were grouped together, there was a small number of Jews, but the largest group was Church of England who marched off to their service in the camp cinema. There were no compulsory church parades on Sundays.

I was in the Protestant, Methodist and Baptist group and we found ourselves allocated a rest room with such comfortable armchairs that some gunners fell asleep during the service. One was even snoring so that the kindly, elderly, padre said, "I know you must be tired with all that training, but will someone tell him not to snore so loudly." And the offender received a dig in the ribs.

When the news about the comfort of our rest room got around, it was sufficient to convert Church of England men into Protestants and, as the rest room became crowded, there was a great rush for the armchairs. And naturally, we *genuine* Protestants, etc. resented the *shallow* intruders.

THE CAMP CINEMA

The camp cinema was always packed on Sunday evenings; and on other evenings if a 'western' or adventure film was being shown. The American star Alan Ladd and the British actress Patricia Roc were particularly popular. When a serial called The Mystery Riders began to be shown, we cheered the hero, Johnny Mack Brown, and booed the villain, Noah Beery. But, as the weeks passed, we changed our loyalty! A dotted line on the screen indicated an underground tunnel, between a shed and the rear room of the saloon, and anticipating this, the audience stamped their feet and shouted, "We want the dotted line." And a great cheer rang out when the line appeared.

One evening, we could make neither head nor tail of a film and eventually twigged that the reels were being shown out of sequence. This caused an uproar. "How can he be alive when he's already been shot dead?" someone yelled.
"Quiet," bawled a voice of authority. But this didn't prevent a few setting out to seek out the projectionist.

Before going to the cinema one evening, I entered the toilet by the roadside. It was in total darkness and when I began to relieve myself, into what I took to be the urinal, I was startled by a yell. A bloke was standing in front of me and he hadn't heard me come in because I was wearing plimsolls!

A short film we saw consisted of a quiz. The gunners yelled out the answers to questions on the screen and, when I got everything right, a colleague was so impressed that, when we were walking back to the barracks together, he urged me to enter one of the radio quizzes.

"You think so?" I replied.

"Absolutely," he confirmed.

"You think I was that good?"

"Sure," he replied.

"Supposing I had already seen the film?" I asked.

As soon as the National Anthem began to be played at the end of a performance, the audience stampeded for the exits. To remedy this, NCOs were stationed at the exits, but, as they were swept aside in the rush, the solution was found by playing the Anthem before the start of the show. This, however, presented a problem for the ever-hungry lads as, with lemonade and NAAFI cakes clutched to their chests, they couldn't stand upright.

PRANKS

Although the cookhouse meals were reasonably good, there were one or two habitual moaners and Gunner Ferguson, a former private school boy, even had his mother provide food for his breakfasts. This same chap and I had a bit of a punch up when I found him with a foot on my bed, cleaning his boots. We were entangled on the floor, with his mate about to come to his rescue, when my pals Terry Smith and Leonard 'Taffy' Rowsell entered the hut. And Ferguson never made that mistake again.

Returning to the hut one Sunday afternoon, I found the occupants, including Terry and Taffy, lounging about and, although there was no space between the beds, my bed was missing. Searching around, I found the mattress under the one on another bed, but could not locate the bed.

Eventually, I went outside and, looking up, there it was on the sloping roof and tied to the chimney. The jokers then had a good laugh, but although they had gone to a lot of trouble to play the prank, they sportingly helped me to rescue the bed. Pranks added sparkle to barrack room life and had to be accepted with good humour.

Prior to 'lights out' at 2230, one of our number secured one end of a strong length of thread to the light switch so that he could pull it into the 'on' position from his bed. NCOs on picket duty went from hut to hut to see that we conformed and, calling "Lights out", a bombardier entered our hut and flicked off the switch. But, as he was barely halfway down the path when the light went on again, he charged back in, expecting to catch the culprit. Finding everyone in bed, he again switched off the light, which came on yet again as soon as he stepped out the door. Once more, he entered the hut, but this time with a smile on his face. "OK, lads. That's the end of it," he said, broke the thread and left us in darkness.

'Lights out' had to be adhered to whether you were in bed or not and, when Terry, Taffy and I were caught preparing for bed with the lights on at 2330 hours, we were ordered to report to the Sergeants' Mess during the next three evenings. Owing to a commitment to throw a cricket ball in a sports' competition, I did only two stints of the duties allocated by Sgt. Sharples, but the others had no such excuse.

I don't know if he regarded it as a prank, but a gunner from the Western Isles claimed that he could tell our fortunes by reading the palms of our hands. Several were told that they had a rosy future, but one wouldn't live to forty and I wasn't to see sixty-five. Not long after the palm-reading session, money was stolen from a wallet left lying on a bed and the fortuneteller became the prime suspect. *(Eric died in November 2017 at the age of 88).*

FATIGUES

Fatigue duties, which might or might not be given as punishment, were, of course, part of the normal routine and would involve such chores as picking up waste paper, sweeping out the cinema and all sorts of jobs, including cleaning and polishing mess tins. When Jeff Buttery was detailed to clean an office, I stood in for him for half-a-dollar/2/6d! (12½p).

LEAVE

Towards the end of July, I was given five days' leave. My parents and my brother, Ian, were on holiday in Galashiels so I joined them there and the kindly owner of the Kings Hotel made a reduction because I was a soldier.

When given a 72-hour pass, I decided to try to hitch hike home. Scotch Corner was reputed to be the best place to obtain a lift, but I went to a spot north of Darlington. In no time at all, a single motorist picked me up, but, unfortunately, he was going only as far as Newcastle. Nevertheless, he was keen to help and when, as we were passing through Gateshead, he spotted a stationary lorry with 'Edinburgh' on it, he drew in beside it. As there was a pub close by, we deduced that was where the driver was likely to be and, when I left the car to enter it, the motorist said he'd wait to see how I got on.

The pub was quite busy so that I called out, "Excuse me, who's the driver of that big lorry outside?"

"I am," said a broad man at the bar.

"Any chance of a lift to Edinburgh? I asked.

"Sure," he replied, "but we're going to Glasgow first."

As Edinburgh was nearer to Dundee, I hesitated briefly before saying, "OK," but there was yet another stumbling block to come.

"Only one thing." said the driver, "That's my mate over there so that there's no room in the cabin and you'll have to stretch out under the canvas at the back."

This was too much. Bouncing about on a hard surface all the way to Edinburgh, via Glasgow, on a cold night was not my idea of fun. "No thanks." I replied, "I've changed my mind."

To which his comment was, "You soldiers are soft these days."

I abandoned the idea of trying to reach Dundee and my motorist friend drove me into Newcastle where I spent four nights in the YMCA and ate excellent meals at the NAAFI. I enjoyed visiting the Industrial Museum and the riverside market, where I saw an escapologist and a man swallowing glass and a watch.

On returning from leave, we all related our various stories as we sat round the stove and one gunner had us all laughing when he told of meeting a man on a train who had asked where he was stationed.

"Barnard Castle," replied the gunner.

"I was stationed there once," said the man. "We were billeted in the Castle."

This is what made us laugh, because, as I've already said, the Castle was a 12th century ruin.

One of my pals spoke in his sleep and answered when someone spoke to him. At first, it was funny, but, when the questioner began to act like a psychiatrist and ask very personal questions, I put a stop to it. Thankfully, this was never repeated and I didn't tell my pal what had happened. In a barrack room full of soldiers, it was inevitable that some would snore, but we led too active a life to be kept awake by snoring.

DARLINGTON, STOCKTON AND REDCAR

Some Saturdays we went to Darlington and, when Terry, Taffy, John Spreadbury, Douglas Ferguson and I came upon a roller-skating rink in South Park, we hired skates and had a go. We had all ice-skated, but this was new to us and we had great fun - whizzing round to music provided by loudspeakers. From Darlington, we would hitchhike to Stockton-on-Tees and back and, on one occasion, the couple, who gave us a lift back, gave us their 'phone number if we wanted a lift to Scarborough the following Saturday. In Stockton, we saw Robert Brothers' circus, spent an evening at the greyhound racing and danced at the NAAFI.

One Saturday, two of us hitch hiked to Redcar and, after we unexpectedly met two others from the camp, the four of us spent the afternoon in an amusement arcade. As evening approached, we wondered where we would spend the night but, as one gunner couldn't afford even the cheapest boarding house, we decided to stick together and sleep in a shelter on the prom. It had been warm and sunny during the day, but, by midnight, it was perishing; with a cold breeze blowing off the North Sea. We huddled together for warmth, but no-one slept and it was a very long night. As soon as daylight appeared we ran along the beach to warm up and, when we saw a beachcomber, we had a go at that, without success. Fortunately, we had enough money to buy a breakfast before separating into the original two pairs. My pal and I then managed a hitchhike to Darlington where we had a nice meal in the NAAFI before returning to camp by truck. Utterly exhausted, we were in bed well before 'lights out' that night.

MAP READING

Map reading was an integral part of our course and, having been told to rendezvous at a certain point, a lorry took us to moor land and dropped us off, one by one, at one-mile intervals. Taffy and I had arranged to meet up so that I walked forward for half a mile while he walked back over the same distance. We then sat down to work out the way to go, but, finding that we disagreed as to the point we had to make for, Taffy convinced me his was the right one and we set off across the undulating moor.

We had not expected to see a soul, but came across a smallholding where a man and woman were busy hoeing. Taffy asked if the reservoir was near, but, as the man didn't seem to understand the question, I laid out the map and pointed to the blue patch. This struck a cord and he uttered, "Ah, Big Watter."
"Yes," we said, Big Water." And the man then pointed out the direction.
"How far?" I asked.
"Not far," he replied.

We thanked the couple, set off again and, after two hours rough going, reached the reservoir. And, very pleased that we were the first to arrive, we stretched out to await the others.

Doubt began to assail us when time passed and no-one appeared. We checked the map reference and found that it was Taffy who was wrong. We had put miles on our journey and there was nothing for it, but to trudge the whole, long, way back to camp.

It was late when we got back to camp and, in answer to our knocking at his door, our sergeant appeared; devoid of tunic and displaying his white braces. "We're back, sergeant," I murmured sheepishly. The obvious statement seemed of no importance to him. "I'm just going to bed," he said casually, "You didn't think I'd be sending out a search party for you two, did you?" We went to bed too, but very much more tired and, as we had missed our meal, more hungry than he was.

Our final experience on the moor was in fog; with visibility so reduced that someone commented that it reminded him of The Hound of the Baskervilles. The able lance bombardier in charge wisely decided that we should all stay together and, sending two gunners to walk just ahead of us, he kept a compass bearing on them as we moved cautiously forward. This bombardier, from Bury St. Edmonds, had the ability to memorise squares and square roots of numbers and was a man we respected. And, like all the Tech. Ack. instructors, he was never aggressive.

REJECTED

About a month after my arrival at Deerbolt Camp, I applied to be considered for a commission. This meant going before a War Office Selection Board (WOSB and spoken of as WOSBY), but the initial steps were being accepted and put forward by, first, a Captain and then the CO. Two others also applied and the Captain accepted all three of us.

I had left school at fifteen with the Junior Leaving Certificate, but, having attended evening classes three nights a week since then, I also had National Certificates – all, of course, Scottish qualifications. The Captain appeared to think these were adequate and was particularly enthusiastic that I had been in the Boys' Brigade.

A week later, we were called for interview by the CO. The tall chap, whom I had found cleaning his boots over my bed and who had attended a private school, was called in first. And ten minutes later departed smiling as he had been accepted. The second interviewee was a burly fellow whose father, I believe, was a Labour M.P. When he came out, he shook his head at me to indicate his rejection. It was, therefore, with some trepidation that I entered the room.

The CO sat at a desk with his back to the window and, on being told to sit down in the chair in front of the desk, I had the sun in my eyes. The Captain was also present and gave me an encouraging smile. But it didn't take the CO long to reject me and his parting words were "You'll make very good non-commissioned officer."

No doubt the CO was influenced by the educational background of the successful candidate, but, as the latter was certainly not the best Tech. Ack., it would appear that the Army put more store on formal education than on intelligence.

One gunner certainly had the right pedigree to become an officer as his father held a high rank in the Army. This, however, went, not in his favour, but against him, as he was 'picked on' by the NCOs. The poor chap had quite a facial growth and, to satisfy them, he had to shave twice a day. Such treatment caused him to hate the Army and those on picket duty round the perimeter of the camp were told to watch out for him, in case he tried to abscond.

One day, I was called to the Battery office to be told that my posting to train as glider pilot had come through. I had made no such application and it was subsequently found that the fellow who had applied had my surname, MALCOLM, as his first name.

A SPECIAL PARADE

The whole regiment was assembled on the parade ground in readiness to receive a visiting Brigadier. It was a hot sunny day and, when, after an hour, the visitor had still not appeared, there was misery in the ranks and two gunners were carted off. In order to keep from fainting, I kept my eyes moving, but, although this helped, I suddenly felt I was going to pass out and asked the Sergeant Major's permission to leave. And, with permission granted, I marched smartly to my hut.

Minutes later, another gunner came in and lay down on his bed. "They're dropping like flies out there," he said, "but nobody else is being allowed to leave the way we did." I never saw the Brigadier, but if/when he did arrive, the ranks would be closed to greet him.

ANOTHER REJECTION AND AWOL

My intake was issued with travel warrants and 10-day leave passes; beginning Friday, 12th September. I didn't go directly home, but broke my journey at Edinburgh to see my brother who was studying for a higher certificate at Leith Nautical College. Ian met me at Waverley Station and took me to his lodgings in Constitution Street, Leith, where Mrs. Brown, his landlady, kindly provided meals and I shared Ian's bed. The next morning, we went to the top of the Scott Monument and into John Knox's House, St Giles and Holyrood Palace, before I caught the 2.30pm train to Dundee.

A surprise awaited me in Dundee, as my father handed me a telegram the minute I stepped inside the door of the house at about 5.30pm. I had submitted an application to join the Royal Army Education Corps and the telegram, sent just two hours after I had left the camp on Friday, read 'RETURN TO UNIT 2359 HOURS 15 SEPTEMBER 47 FOR RAEC INTERVIEW = OC 193 BATTERY'. I left Dundee at 11am on Monday morning, was back in Deerbolt Camp by about 6pm and, on reporting to Acting BSM Kerr the following morning, was detailed to clean the washhouses!

The interviews were being held in York on the Wednesday. I was up at 5.30am and, together with eight or nine others, arrived there at 9.30am. And as we had some time to kill, we wandered about the old town and climbed York Minster before coming across an Army barracks displaying the sign DEMOBILISATION CENTRE. On strolling in to have a look, another sign directed us to the dining hall where we found ladies in white overalls waiting to serve in the otherwise deserted hall. And, as soon as we approached, they piled copious helpings on to plates and we sat down to a good meal.

A sergeant then appeared and, after enquiring if we had enjoyed our meal, he asked if there was anything else he could do for us. "Yes," said one of our number, "Any ciggies, Sarg.?"
"Sorry, boys," he replied, "That's one thing I don't have."
We thanked him and, on leaving the premises, took to our heels. "Do you think we could have been demobbed if we'd stayed?" someone asked.
"More likely court-martialled," replied another."

I think the interviewees were seen alphabetically as I had to wait for some time before being called into a large room where nine officers sat behind a long table. "Why do you want to join the Education Corps?" asked the Lieut. Colonel, President of the Selection Board.
"I feel I could be useful to the Corps, sir."
"Why is that?"
"I have qualifications in a number of subjects. After leaving school, I continued studying at evening classes and have National Certificates."
"Have you had any teaching experience?"
"No, sir." (Perhaps I should not have been so honest!)
"We require personnel who have a knowledge of teaching. I suggest that you reapply in three or four months' time."

The interview was over, but I said, "Excuse me, sir, I have a question."

"Yes?"

"How can I acquire teaching experience during the three or four month period?"

"When you return to your unit, I want you to ask the Education Officer to allow you to get this experience."

"You may not be aware of it, sir, but education at my camp consists of a film and the tutor disappears during the showing."

It was obvious that my statement shocked the panel and, after a brief silence, the Chairman said, "Reapply as I have suggested."

I have no idea if any of the others were selected, but certainly no-one appeared downhearted. As for me, an attraction of the Education Corps was that their training centre was at Loch Lomond, but I never did reapply. I had been issued with another travel warrant and so returned to Dundee directly from York

During my leave, when I called at Thos. Bonar's office to see my old work mates, Mr Lorimer, a senior director, engaged me in a friendly chat and said that he looked forward to my return. Then, as I was leaving, he attempted to put a £1 note into my hand and, when I refused it, he thrust it at me saying, "Then buy your mother a bunch of flowers."

After an enjoyable leave, I returned to Deerbolt at 6pm on Friday, 26 September to be told, at the guardhouse, that I was under open arrest for being absent without official leave (AWOL) for two days. Next day, when I explained to Sgt. Kerr that I taken the ten days granted to me and that the additional two had been due to the interview, he took the matter to Major Barton. And the Major must have been a decent man, as I heard no more about the matter. This made me the hero of the barrack room that evening – two days late and got away with it!

FINAL EXAMS

Our heads were full of the theory of ballistics and its practical use in gunnery, and, with the exams imminent, our bookie's runner made a list of our names and gave various odds on each of us coming first. But he was on a losing wicket as we all knew that this honour would go to Gunner Price and not a bet was placed. Alan Price, with whom I later corresponded, told me he came from a large family and that, although we were paid only 19/0d (95p)[1] a week, he had never been as well off as he was in the Army. The latter circumstance applied to most of us and, certainly, to me. But I was particularly fortunate in having a mother who didn't spend the seven shillings a week that I allotted to her and banked it for me.

The computation test suited me and, although John Spreadbury handed in his completed paper before I did, he had made an error while I had everything correct. We were given map coordinates and had to set up an artillery board in fifteen minutes, with penalties imposed for time overran. Shortly after beginning, I discovered an error, erased my figures and began again. Engaged in the second set of calculations, I raised my head to find that the others were all working on the opposite side of their

---

[1] National Health Insurance contributions and a 10d (about 4p) clothing allowance were deducted from this and, for some unknown reason, I had got £1 in Perth.

sheets to where I was. This made me realize that I was wrong again so that, once more, I applied the eraser and started on a third attempt. Most of the others submitted their results within the time limit, but although I was one minute late, the invigilator remarked that he had never before seen anyone set up three artillery boards in sixteen minutes! Although I passed well in every subject, it didn't, in retrospect, matter a tinker's cuss whether I passed the course or not. Tech. Acks. were required only in Field Artillery and, as I was posted to a Heavy Anti-Aircraft Battery, my acquired skills were never put to use.

MILTON BARRACKS, GRAVESEND, KENT

On completion of the Tech. Ack. course, Terry and Taffy were posted to Orsett, near Grays, in Essex, while Jack Jarvis and Sam Lodge, from Squad 70B, and I went to 278 Battery, 75 Heavy Anti-Aircraft (HAA and spoken of as Heavy Ack Ack) Regiment at Milton Barracks, Gravesend. Sam, who was the only man I met with the same Canadian style uniform which I had, told me that he had been issued with brown boots on enlistment and ordered to blacken them.

It was Thursday 20 November, 1947 when, laden with kit bags and other paraphernalia, Jack, Sam and I travelled by rail to London's Kings Cross Station. We then had to take the Underground to another mainline station, for the final part of the journey to Gravesend, and were surprised to find it deserted until the penny dropped. It was the wedding day of Princess Elizabeth and Philip Mountbatten.

By late afternoon, we were installed in 'A'-Troop hut at Milton Barracks; among somewhat rougher men who were shortly to be demobbed and had apparently served for only eighteen months. I believe their Demobilization Number was 78 and that this was the last batch to receive demob suits and gratuities. I think that there were no demob numbers between 78 and 101, but all attempts to verify this have failed, and, similar to Jack and Sam, my group number was 111. The following day, we were interposted into a 'B' troop hut, but, although with a better bunch than in 'A' troop, I missed my colleagues at Deerbolt.

FATHERLY ADVICE

Similar to almost all our senior NCOs, Battery Sergeant Major Hill, who spoke to us shortly after our arrival, wore campaign ribbons of the Second World War. "There are plenty of nice girls in the town," he said, "Keep clear of the others."

I was appointed to his clerical staff which was a busy one; dealing with pay, leave passes, travel warrants, orders for notice boards, etc. When a leave pass and a travel warrant were issued to the BSM himself, we learned that he would be away for ten days. But, although the destination on the warrant was in Northern Ireland, he was seen in a nearby town with a young lady on his arm who, rumoured had it, was not his wife. This aroused speculation as to how the travel warrant was used. With his name on it, did he still manage to flog it or did he use it after a few days with his girlfriend?

Not wanting an office job, I asked the BSM to release me, but he was reluctant to do so and said, "You're the best clerk we've ever had." And, knowing that all the others had no clerical experience, I replied, "I'm the *only* clerk you've ever had." It was a struggle, but eventually he agreed to my return to the squad.

DARTFORD AND LECTURES

On Tuesday, 13 January, 1948, I learned from the notice board that I was going on a cadre course for potential NCOs which began, in Dartford, the next day. The participants travelled to Dartford roughly three days a week till 2 February and at the end of the course, which included such topics as Control Room Operating, Command Post Work, Words of Command and How To Give A Lecture, I got 82% in the written exam and came out on top.

A few days later, all those who had been on the course were ordered to give two lectures to the men; the first on any subject and the second on a prescribed one. Having read a book about the Amazon Region, I chose 'THE AMAZING AMAZON' for my first subject and began – "In spite of the many attempts to master it, Brazil retains much of its ancient secrecy and mystery…." This got me off to a good start and, at the conclusion of the lecture, a young subaltern asked when I had visited Brazil. "Never," I replied.
To which his response was, "Well, I have and you know more about it than I do."

Rumours were always rife and when this handsome officer got what seemed to be a rather sudden posting, it was said to be because he had been caught in bed with an ATS girl. And when, sometime later, a girl was reputed to have come to the barrack gate looking for the father of her baby, there was speculation as to who would be posted next.

My second lecture was on the prescribed subject, 'GO TO BEARING', which dealt with the degrees on a compass. In order to see that they were paying attention, the audience was required to answer questions and, when I asked, "In which direction is 180°?" several hands shot up. Now, among those electing to answer was Gunner X who was noted for his lack of mental capacity. And, although the audience thought that nobody in their right mind would chose him, I did and he called out "Due south". There was a moment's silence. An officer in the front row raised an eyebrow while another smiled. "Correct," I replied, and continued as if nothing untoward had occurred.

After the lecture, I was asked by a friend why I had chosen Gunner X. "He gave the correct answer, didn't he?", I said.
"Yes," said my friend, "but that was luck."
"Not at all," I replied, but as I could see he was puzzled, I went on to enlighten him.
"Last night," I said, "I told Gunner X that, no matter what I asked him, he was to say 'due south' and went over this with him at least a dozen times." But as it had been Gunner X's one moment of glory, I asked my friend to keep this between ourselves.

STIFFKEY AND PROMOTION

Some weeks later, I was sent for by Major Finch, our Battery Commander and a pleasant officer who dressed in a somewhat casually fashion. "Would you be willing to go on a predictor course?" he asked. And when I expressed agreement, said, "The course is at The Norfolk Training Centre in Stiffkey. It lasts for three weeks and being a qualified Tech. Ack. you should do well. A bombardier and a sergeant from the other batteries are going and, if you do well, I'll have you a sergeant within six months." It was with a feeling of exhilaration that I left the office: promotion on the horizon and guaranteed by the Battery Commander himself!

Laden with full pack, I travelled to Stiffkey on 17 March and was lodged in a hut with others on the same course. Classes were held daily from 0815 to1230 and from1330 to1615 with the times divided into subject periods. Captain Dick was the principal gunnery instructor and his assistant was Sgt. Major Butchard. Captain Dick was always smartly dressed, spoke with authority and wore the red band of the Staff College on his cap. And, as he seemed to typify the leading character in the nightly radio programme, 'Dick Barton, Special Agent', I always thought of him as Dick Barton.

Similar to Deerbolt, we were issued with notebooks which bore, on the front cover, the printed letters S.O. Book 135 (at the top), a crown between the letters GR (in the middle) and (in a box) SUPPLIED FOR THE PUBLIC SERVICE. And printed sheets were issued to cover the lectures and practical work.

When gazing out of the window one afternoon, I received a dig in the ribs from the gunner sitting next to me who then whispered that I had been asked to define the gunnery term 'angle of departure'. I looked up to find the Captain staring in my direction, but, having been well trained at Deerbolt, I was able to give the correct answer.

There were three cookhouses on the camp and, on one occasion, I tried to have the same meal in each of them. I managed two, but as the cookhouses were some distance apart, I arrived at the third one as it was closing and was told, "Too bad, mate."

When, for some reason, we were free from Thursday the 25th until Wednesday the 31st, I hitch hiked to Norwich where I had bed and breakfast at the Salvation Army Hostel and other meals in the NAAFI. And in addition to seeing the sites of Norwich, I went on two coach tours. One was a Mystery Tour, which lived up to its name and turned out to be to Lowestoft and Great Yarmouth, and the other was to Whipsnade Zoo in Bedfordshire.

The tour to Lowestoft and Great Yarmouth has remained more in my memory because, after visiting Lowestoft fog came rolling in from the North Sea. It was, therefore, with great difficulty that the driver got us into Great Yarmouth where he announced, "We'll stop here for three quarters of an hour. There's a café across the road and, if you feel your feet getting wet, you're heading in the wrong direction." We cautiously crossed over to the café, recrossed after refreshments, and saw nothing of Great Yarmouth. Fog continued to blot out most of the scenery during the return journey and, as we alighted from the coach in Norwich, the driver assured us that it was normally a nice tour! At the end of the course, we were tested on general gunnery terminology, procedure, cable layout, data flow types of transmission and electrical devices. The tests were of a multiple-choice type and as penalties were imposed for wrong answers, guesswork could lead to a negative mark. I did reasonably well, but Captain Dick said that he thought I would have done better. Back in Milton Barracks, Major Finch said he was pleased with my result and repeated that he'd have me a sergeant within six months.

On returning from leave a fortnight later, I found my mates addressing me as 'bomb'. My first stripe had come through and I had Major Finch's word that I'd have the second one in a matter of weeks. But I had barely become used to being a lance bombardier when the axe fell. Major Finch was posted and it was rumoured that he had been demoted to Captain. He was replaced by Major Grubb and Grubb stopped all promotion. And when, months later, a bombardier, without my knowledge of gunnery, was posted to our battery, I knew I'd remain a lance bombardier no matter how many courses I passed. This changed my attitude to the Army: from then on, I would enjoy the life and confine my studies to subjects that would benefit me in civvy street.

ANOTHER INDOOR JOB

Between the course at Dartford and the one at Stiffkey, I had a few weeks on the telephone switchboard in the barracks and, as it was a cold winter, this was a comfortable and cushy number. It was very gratifying to sit at ease, enjoying the warmth of a coal fire, while deriving the additional pleasure from seeing my less fortunate colleagues being drilled outside.

My sole companion on the exchange was Gunner Ralph Leighton and, when we were sitting doing little or nothing one afternoon, he said, "Do you know what would make this perfect?"

"What?" I asked.

"Toast," he replied. "Too bad, eh?"

After a moment's thought, I said, "Hold the fort. I'll be back in ten minutes," and headed for the cookhouse.

Apart from the corporal who emerged from behind the ovens as I approached the counter, the cookhouse was empty. "What do *you* want?" he aggressively asked, and when I said, "Bread and margarine", he brusquely ordered me out. Knowing that he received regular calls from a girlfriend, I raised my hands in resignation and said, "OK, but remember I'm on the switchboard and we control *all* calls in and out of the camp." I was on my way to the door when he called me back and grudgingly handed over the items to make Ralph's afternoon perfect. The camp cooks were a mixed lot but, under the guidance of NCOs, they generally provided satisfactory meals. And knowing them personally was a decided advantage when you were looking for a second helping. Toast was occasionally made in our hut at night by raking out the fire and placing the bread on the glowing embers.

Ralph was rather a good artist who, during quiet periods, would pass the time by either sketching women in various modes of dress or talking to a girl telephonist at the town's exchange. To facilitate his conversations with the latter, he had one of our lines permanently connected to her and this almost led to his demise as a telephonist. He would deal with a camp call, chat to the girl, deal with a camp call, chat to the girl and this could go on for hours. But the day came when he was shaken out of his complacency as the irate voice of the girl's superior came through the phones threatening to report him to the CO. From hearing the start of the CO's conversations with his friends, we learned that his nickname was Squeak!

When Ralph and I were bored, we would say to each other, "What time is it?" and then ring up the GPO's Talking Clock. But we had no need of an alarm clock as the girls at the Gravesend Exchange gave us a morning call. We would arrange blind dates for these girls, but, as their dulcet voices did not always match their appearance, this could bring complaints from some of the lads. The girls, of course, must have suffered similar disappointments.

On learning that a young sergeant was keen on dating, we told him to come to see us at the exchange. There was an extension phone in the corner of the room and we told him to lift the receiver and to ask for Margaret when I gave the signal. After dialling the number at the switchboard, I called out "Now" and, on lifting the receiver, the hopeful sergeant said, "Can I speak to Margaret, please?" With our eyes on him, we watched his expression change to one of astonishment as what he heard was an operator saying "Buckingham Palace. Buckingham Palace." The sergeant slammed down the receiver, but, although he proved to be a good sport, he never again asked us to provide him with a date! Life on the switchboard was certainly cushy, but the few weeks I had on it were enough for me and I was off to Stiffkey anyway.

NOT THEFT

As coal remained rationed in Britain for something like ten years after the Second World War, the Army did its best to conserve stocks. Our barrack room was heated by a coal fire and the weekly ration was barely adequate so that, if we were too generous to the fire at the beginning of the week, we shivered towards the end of it.

The winter of 1947/48 was a very cold one and it was, therefore, a godsend when men of our hut were detailed to deliver coal throughout the camp, including the married quarters. There was great activity around the coal lorry when it stopped outside our hut and, while the official supply was being unloaded and tipped, under supervision, into the hut's bunker, *our man* passed massive lumps into waiting hands. The lumps were then hidden in such places as our metal lockers and used first to dispose of the evidence. The acquisition was not regarded as theft, but a means of survival and everyone participated.

SEEING THE LIGHT

On the first Church Parade, one gunner, whose Service Book bore the word ATHEIST, stood apart. "Don't worry," said the Sergeant Major, "we have a place for you too." And sent him to the cookhouse to peel spuds. This resulted in the atheist adopting a religion for all future occasions.

GRAYS, ESSEX

As my two Deerbolt pals, Terry Smith and Taffy Rowsell, were stationed at Orsett, I arranged to meet them in Grays. I crossed on the Gravesend Ferry and we ate in a tearoom where the service was diabolical and the waitress ignored our attempts to pay the bill. Having waited for about fifteen minutes, we headed for the door. And the waitress was on to us like a shot.

Returning from another visit to Grays, I arrived at the ferry terminal to find that all crossings to Gravesend were cancelled due to fog on the river. However, when I was still hanging about on the jetty, I was surprised to hear voices and, looking down, saw four or five people in a small motorboat. "Hello there." I shouted, "Are you going over?" The answer was in the affirmative and, as I was in uniform which no doubt helped, they agreed to take me.

After I had descended the vertical iron ladder and found a seat among the others, the boat cast off into the gloom. And with foghorns wailing around us, we were about halfway across the river when a large ship loomed out of the murk. In our small craft, it was quite frightening for the minute or two that she towered over us before disappearing upstream. We all knew that we had had a narrow escape and were greatly relieved to land at Gravesend.

DENNING

When Denning first joined the regiment, he said to me, "The officers at my last camp thought me stupid so I'll see to it that this lot think the same." And he kept his word. If he was told to carry out an order, he would do so, providing nothing strenuous, such as an assault course, was involved. Most certainly, in any group activity, the group he was in would be the last to finish. As the fit fellows found it impossible to heave him up and over a brick wall, they told him to walk round it.

One day, Denning was in a running party, watched by officers from a distance, and, when only halfway round the first circuit of the playing field, I saw that he was already out of puff. "Get behind the shed," I called out to him. The rest of us closed up to conceal his disappearance and he slipped back among us during the final circuit.

Apart from those who were boxers, it was difficult to get volunteers for the inter-battery boxing competition, as even the hard men were unwilling to accept punishment to amuse others. It therefore came as a shock to learn from the notice board that the cumbersome and non-athletic Denning had chosen to represent us.

He wasn't seen much during the week preceding the competition and rumour had it that he was training for the big event. Other speculation was that he would report 'sick', he'd go down in the first round or might reach the second if his opponent breaks both his arms. Apart from the contestants, no-one took the competition seriously and there was great hilarity in our battery about Denning's participation.

When the big day arrived, the regiment poured into the gymnasium and it was soon 'standing room only'. An experienced NCO physical training instructor acted as referee and the judges, sitting at a table by the ringside, were the CO and two other officers. Aggressive lighter weights, the first contestants, were soon knocking each other about, encouraged by an enthusiastic audience. But, for us, the highlight of the evening began when Denning stepped into the ring and, with clasped hands raised above his head, acknowledged the deafening roars of support from the men of his battery. His opponent was taller and well built. The referee gave them the usual warnings. They touched gloves and went to their corners.

The cheers died away at the sound of the bell, which signified the commencement of Round One, and both boxers took up defensive stances in the centre of the ring. Denning's opponent made a jab which merely glanced off Denning's shoulder, but he dropped to the floor and lay there to the count of eight. He then rose, with little effort and to a great cheer, to confront his opponent again. But, when a straight right to the body again sent Denning to the floor to the count of eight, the CO was on his feet shouting, "This is a boxing match. For God's sake, mix it."

The expression on the face of Denning's opponent was one of bewilderment. He lashed out at Denning's face, but, although he hit fresh air, Denning once more dropped to the boards and lay spread-eagled. It was all too much for the irate CO and, again out of his chair, he shouted, "Get out of the ring. Get out."

Although Denning's *fight* was the main topic of conversation in the camp that night, the central figure did not participate, but was seen striding past the guardhouse gate in his best uniform. Apparently the small print in the notice asking for volunteers had intimated that participants would get a 72-hour pass. And Denning had read the small print!

EDUCATIONAL VISITS

As it relieved us of other duties, educational visits were popular and, on seeing a large group about to board a coach, bound for Canterbury, I hurried to the Battery Office to seek permission to go. "You've just returned from leave," accused the BSM, but, after refusing permission, he added that I could join the next tour.

On an educational visit to the Royal Mint, in London, the pleasant gentleman who escorted us round, explained that, when the minted coins were moved from one section to another, they were weighed and not counted. And, with a smile, he assured us that theft from the establishment was impossible. Moving on from the penny to the half-crown section, our guide scooped up a handful of half-crowns, handed one to each of us and went on to talk about the value of old coins before he began retrieving the half-crowns. The smile on his face was then replaced by one of astonishment. "I gave out ten," he expostulated, "Where's the missing one?" He counted us and there were only nine!

One of our party had wandered ahead of us. The guide called him back and on holding out his hand and saying, "The coin?", the gunner withdrew the half-crown from his trouser pocket. "Did you think you were getting it to keep?" enquired the again smiling guide. The foolish expression on the face of the culprit showed that this was indeed the case, but he wasn't the only one who had formed the same impression.

Other visits were to the Houses of Parliament (which I'd previously visited with my parents), Lambeth Central Fire Station and the Ford Motor Company's works, in Dagenham. At Lambeth, we learned that they had dealt with 2380 flying bombs and 511 rockets during the war and, at Ford's, who provided us with refreshments at the end of the tour, we saw the assembly line system which produced a car every minute.

A FIRESIDE SOLDIER AND A POTENTIAL DUST-UP

Although the expiry date was clearly shown on a leave pass, some had to be *told* the day they had to return. There was an instance, however, when a gunner returned to the camp three days early. At first, he would not satisfy our curiosity as to why, but eventually spilled the beans. His father, a former soldier who had seen much foreign service, had called him 'a fireside soldier' and this had resulted in an argument which was the reason for his early return.

Most of us would have laughed at the so-called insult, but this gunner had a short temper and, although small, was proud of his strength. Every day, he used chest expanders and had no difficulty in lifting the 56 lb shells of the Heavy Ack Ack guns. One of his pastimes was throwing a knife at the door of the barrack room and this may have been the cause of the brawl he had with a roommate whom he would have strangled if others had not intervened. Generally, however, he gave little trouble.

It was always important to stand up for yourself and, one day, prior to my promotion, I was washing myself at one of the sinks at the door of our hut, when the shaving mirror which I had borrowed and was about to use, disappeared. I hadn't seen who had taken it, but, as Gunner Williams was proceeding towards the bathhouse, I followed him in and saw the mirror beside where he stood. Williams was a muscular Welsh coalminer, but, when I repossessed the article saying, "If you want the mirror, ask for it," he raised no objection.

Williams and I never differed on any subsequent occasion and it is to my regret that I let him down regarding a photo which he lent to me, prior to demob. It was a picture of a group of us and I was to return it to his home address, but, unfortunately, I lost the address.

BRADY

Brady, a Scot, was a very different character – he *was* trouble and all ranks treated him with caution. In battlefield conditions, he may well have been a hero but, due to his aggressive behaviour, nobody gave him a direct order. My first experience of this was when Sgt. 'Cannonball' Conner had us lined up and noticed Brady was missing. "Where's Brady?" he asked.
"In the NAAFI[2]," was the gleeful answer.
"Well, go and tell him to get up here," he ordered a gunner. On his return from the NAAFI, the gunner reported, "Brady says he's coming." Yet, although it was

---

[2] The acronym for Navy, Army and Air Force Institutes which ran the canteens.

another half-hour before Brady arrived, Cannonball, did not reprimand him.

Brady never disobeyed an order and worked well enough in the ranks. But when things were on a personal footing, it was a different matter and he was unpredictable. When an Other Ranks' dance was being held in the gymnasium one evening, Brady was not allowed in because he was drunk. This caused him to create such a scene at the door that two RPs (Regimental Policemen) intervened. When the first one approached him from behind, Brady turned and struck him to the ground. And, when the second then came at him, Brady knocked him about somewhat before he suddenly stopped fighting and was marched to the guardhouse.

Up in front of the CO next day, Brady stated that he was sorry for what happened. He also stated that, as it was dark and he was attacked from behind, he didn't know it was a regimental policeman and he had merely defended himself. The CO, however, was not in the dark. Brady was sent to Aldershot glasshouse and his demob number changed from 106 to 110, so that he had to remain longer in the Army.

The spell in the glasshouse had no affect whatsoever on Brady and, towards of end of May, 1949, he knocked out a sergeant, beat up a lance jack and badly injured a gunner, when drunk. For this, he received a much longer sentence, but I don't know if his demob number was changed for a second time.

DESCRIPTION OF MAN.

Date of birth 5 · 5 · 29

Height 5 ft. 11 ins.

Colour of eyes Blue Grey

Colour of hair Brown

If before you are called up for service you have any serious illness or serious accident, or have reason to think there has been a deterioration in your health, you should immediately inform the Local Office of the Ministry of Labour and National Service whose address appears on the back of your registration form N.S.2, giving full particulars, including any medical evidence you can supply, and quoting your Registration No. and other entries made on form N.S.2, so that the information can be considered before an enlistment notice is issued to you.

* If this Certificate is lost or mislaid, the fact must be at once reported.

The finder should send it to the nearest Local Office of the Ministry of Labour and National Service.

(8/45) M61460 200M 1/46 CN&Co 749 (6226) 8

NATIONAL SERVICE ACTS

GRADE CARD

Registration No. DML29656

Mr. Eric McR McMillen

whose address on his registration card is

219 Blackness Road

Dundee

was medically examined on 26 MAR 1947

at ~~GAIRD HALL DUNDEE~~

and placed in

GRADE* II Two

Chairman of Board George W Miller

Medical Board stamp DUNDEE MEDICAL BOARD

Man's Signature

[P.T.O.

*The roman numeral denoting the man's Grade (with number also spelt out) will be entered in RED ink by the Chairman himself e.g., Grade I (one) Grade II (two) (a) (Vision).

N.S. 55.

NATIONAL SERVICE ACTS.

ENLISTMENT NOTICE

MINISTRY OF LABOUR AND NATIONAL SERVICE REGIONAL OFFICE,

21. DOUGLAS CRES.

~~MINISTRY OF LABOUR & NATIONAL SERVICE.
REGIONAL OFFICE.
MILITARY RECRUITING SECTION,~~

EDINBURGH 12

2 1 MAY 1947 ....(Date

MR. *Eric Mc'Q Malcolm*

219 Blackness Road

Dundee

Angus

Registration No. *DM2 29686*

DEAR SIR,

In accordance with the National Service Acts, you are called upon for service in the Territorial Army and are required to present yourself on ....THURSDAY........day

– 5 JUN 1947 (date), between 9 a.m. and 12 noon, or as soon as possible thereafter on that day, to :—

No 42 County Primary Training *Centre/*Win.

GENERAL SERVICE CORPS,

Queen's Barracks

Perth

Perth ....(nearest railway station).

Every endeavour should be made to report between the hours stated above.

* A Travelling Warrant for your journey is enclosed. Before starting your journey you <u>must</u> exchange the warrant for a ticket at the booking office named on the warrant. If possible, this should be done a day or two before you are due to travel. If your warrant is made out to travel from London you may obtain a railway ticket at, and travel from, the most convenient station to your address.

If you have been transferred on or after 1st June, 1940, beyond daily travelling distance from your home by or with the approval of the Ministry of Labour and National Service to work of national importance, and you desire to travel home before you are required to report for service, you may apply for a free travelling warrant for this purpose. If you wish to apply you should go immediately to the nearest Local Office of the Ministry of Labour and National Service, and take with you this enlistment notice *[and the enclosed Travelling Warrant (A/cs. 617)].

A Postal Order for 4s. in respect of advance of service pay, is also enclosed.

Immediately on receipt of this notice, you should inform your employer of the date upon which you are required to report for service.

Yours faithfully,

YOU SHOULD READ CAREFULLY THE NOTES OVERLEAF.

M J Mac MASTER

for *Registrar*

* *Delete* *applies to*

46

NOTES.

1. When you join your Unit you should take with you :—
   This Enlistment Notice,
   The enclosed envelope N.S. 124, completed in accordance with the directions at the top.

   Your
   - Razor
   - Certificate of Registration (N.S.2)
   - Medical Grade Card (N.S. 55)
   - National Registration Identity Card

   All Ration Books, including Clothing Book and *all* unused coupons.

2. Uniform will be issued to you after joining H.M. Forces. Any kit that you take with you should not exceed 15 lbs. in total weight and should be limited to an overcoat, change of underclothes, stout pair of boots, and personal kit, such as hair-brush, tooth-brush, soap and towel.

3. Men joining H.M. Forces are advised not to dispose of any of their civilian clothing, including underclothes, until they have completed at least one month's paid service. A man discharged or released before completion of one month's service does not receive a supplementary issue of clothing coupons.

4. Before you leave to join your Unit you should take or send to, ask your employer to send your Unemployment Book (including Exempt Persons Book) to the nearest Local Office of the Ministry of Labour and National Service. The Local Office should be informed why the book is being surrendered. You should keep a note of the name of the Local Office and the number on the book.

5. If you are sick and unable to travel you must obtain a certificate from your Doctor and send it by post to the Officer Commanding the Unit which you have been ordered to join, at the address given on the Enlistment Notice overleaf. The Officer Commanding may grant you sick leave, so that you can join as soon as you are fit to do so.

6. If circumstances suddenly arise, such as the illness of your wife, or a relative, which make you wish to apply for deferment of joining for a few days, you must write to the Officer Commanding the Unit which you have been ordered to join, giving a full explanation of the circumstances which have arisen and which make it necessary for you to apply to delay your joining. The Officer Commanding may, if he thinks fit, defer your joining for a reasonable period. Deferment cannot be granted on purely business grounds.

7. If you are granted deferment of joining by the Officer Commanding, your travelling warrant should be returned at once to the Ministry of Labour and National Service Office from which it was sent, with a letter giving the reason for its return. You should retain this Enlistment Notice and the Postal Order for four shillings. A fresh travelling warrant, for use when the period of deferment expires, will be issued by the Officer Commanding your Unit. No pay from Army Funds is admissible until you actually join your Unit.

8. You must understand that you will be deemed to have been enlisted from the date on which you are required to present yourself to your Unit and unless you have been granted deferment of joining as explained above, failure to join your Unit on the appointed date will make you an absentee and you will then be liable to be arrested and brought before a Court of Summary Jurisdiction.

Soldier's Service Book.

(Soldier's Pay Book, Army Book 64 (Part II), will be
issued for active service.)

Entries in this book (other than those connected with
the making of a Soldier's Will) are to be made under the
superintendence of an Officer.

Instructions to Soldier.

1. You are held **personally responsible** for the safe
custody of this book.

2. You will always **carry this book** on your person.

3. You must produce the book whenever called upon
to do so by the Civil Police or by a competent military
authority, viz., Officer, Warrant Officer, N.C.O. or Military
Policeman.

4. You must not alter or make any entry in this book
(except as regards your Will on pages 15 to 20).

5. Should you lose the book, you will report the matter
to your immediate military superior.

6. On your transfer to the Army Reserve this book will
be handed into your Orderly Room for transmission,
through the O. i/c Records, to place of rejoining on
mobilization.

7. You will be permitted to retain this book after
discharge, but should you lose the book after discharge it
cannot be replaced.

8. If you are discharged from the Army Reserve, this
book will be forwarded to you by the O. i/c Records.

PARTICULARS OF TRAINING.

Courses and Schools. Specialist Qualifications. Showing result.	Date.	Initials of Officer.
T.O.E.T.S RIFLE PASSED	26/6/47	
L.M.G PASSED	26/6/47	
RIFLE COURSE PART 1 IN P.S. 90/56	1/7/47	
L.M.G. COURSE PART 1 IN P.S.112/49		
GRENADES 2 NO. 36 THROWN		
BASIC EFFICIENCY TESTS	3/7/47	
PASSED PASSED		
COMPLETED PRIMARY TRAINING	5/7/47	

Entry in Service Book on completion of Basic Training.

Shoulder badge and flash

Squad 5, 'A' Company, Queens Barracks, Perth, June, 1947

Back Row: Left to Right. Gow, McGregor, Fortheringham, Coutts, Tennant, Lauder, Hendry, me, Richie and Quigley.
Middle Row: Handlan, Coleman, Pitkeathlie, Ogilvie, Geekie, Newlans, McPherson, Bell, Gray, Leerie and Gellatly.
Front Row: Small, Brown, Gray, Handling, Cpl. McKerracher, Sgt. Smith, L/Cpl. MacMalan, Tom Bamburgh, Lawson and McQuilter.

50

Back row: Alan Price and Reginald Baile.
Front row: Terry Smith, Leonard (Taffy) Rowsell and me.

Taken in Darlington when we were at Deerbolt Camp. Reg Baile and I wear the plastic, grenade, cap badge instead of the metal one.

51

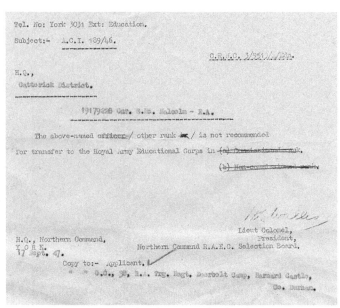

RAEC Selection Board rejection

With parents, Galashiels, 1 Aug., 1947

With Permission to Wear Plain Clothes

PERMANENT PASS

278 H.A.A. BATTERY R.A.

The holder, No 228

Rank .... GNR .... *Name* .... N. H. SCOTT É

(a) *has permission to be absent from his quarters after duty daily until the first parade ordered for the following day, except when on duty.*

(b) *has permission to be absent from his quarters after duty Saturday until first parade ordered for the following Monday morning, except when on duty.*

Signed .... *Major, R.A.*
Commanding 278 H.A.A. Battery R.A.

Gale & Polden Ltd., Aldershot 928-u

The Organ for all Artillerymen—Regular, Territorial and Dominion—
and the Magazine of the R.A. Association.

Price 9d. Post Free 10d.

T^{HE}GUNNER

UBIQUE

QUO FAS ET GLORIA DUCUNT

Vol. XXX, No. 4 — JULY, 1948

HOW'S YOUR FEET?

Painful skin troubles are quickly relieved when you apply Germolene Ointment. Such things as blisters, cuts, foot-rot, sore toes, burns, abrasions and other skin complaints like eczema, pimples, irritating rashes, quickly yield to the soothing, healing touch of Germolene. By penetrating into the skin Germolene draws out dirt and "matter", so relieving inflammation and itching. If you have hot swollen feet bathe them, dry them, and apply Germolene and they'll soon feel cool and comfortable. You will find Germolene a great standby.

IF YOU HAVE SKIN TROUBLE THERE'S ALWAYS

Germolene
ASEPTIC OINTMENT
1/6 and 3/8 including Purchase Tax.
SOLD EVERYWHERE (including N.A.A.F.I.).

KEEP A TIN IN YOUR KIT

On or Off Parade

there's nothing like

CHERRY BLOSSOM
BOOT POLISH

for a brighter shine in half the time

Black, Brown & Tonette. Tins. 3½° & 7°

CHISWICK PRODUCTS LTD. LONDON W.4.

For healthy teeth and sweet breath

Euthymol
TOOTH PASTE

Printed in Great Britain

'Second to None'

GREYS
CIGARETTES

Just honest-to-goodness tobacco

Plain or cork-tipped 'Greys' will always appeal to those smokers who ask of a cigarette that it shall be pleasant and satisfying.

15 for 2/7½

ISSUED BY GODFREY PHILLIPS LIMITED

Advertisements in 'The Gunner'

Bob Shield (left) & me.

Harry Kemp, Derek Dye & me.

Back Row: Left to right: Fred Phipps, Morris Turner, Stan Roberts, Bob Shield, Norman Woolley & Derek Dye.

Middle Row: Ted Ashley, Smith, John Lilley & me.

Front Row: Jack Jarvis & Harry Kemp, Langham Camp, near Stiffkey Firing Camp, 21 Aug., 1948.

Welbeck

THE MAGAZINE OF
ARMY COLLEGE NORTH

WINTER GARDEN THEATRE

DRURY LANE, W.C.2

Licensed by the Lord Chamberlain to RICHARD HERBERT DEWES
Proprietors: WINTER GARDEN THEATRE (LONDON) LTD.

ALBERT DE COURVILLE

presents

MICHAEL MYERBERG'S PRODUCTION

LUTE SONG

by

SIDNEY HOWARD and WILL IRWIN

Music by RAYMOND SCOTT   Lyrics by BERNARD HANIGHEN
Choreography by YEICHI NIMURA and LISAN KAY
Scenery and Costumes by ROBERT EDMOND JONES

Assistant to Producer: *Production Supervisor:*
JOHN PAUL   CLIFFORD GULLIVER

Directed by
ALBERT DE COURVILLE

EVENINGS at 7.0

MATINEES: THURSDAY and SATURDAY at 2.30 p.m.

Royal Artillery Association
Dartford Benevolent Branch

A GRAND DANCE

at the

HORNS CROSS Drill Hall

SATURDAY, 29th JANUARY 1949

Dancing from 7.30 to 11.45 p.m. to

Fully Licensed Bar

RHYTHMIC

Late Buses to Gravesend, Denton, Dartford, Crayford & Erith after the Dance.

SPOT PRIZES and NOVELTIES

ADMISSION 2/6

Complimentary Ticket

THE SALVATION ARMY
RED SHIELD HOSTEL.

Room No. *68*   Bed No.

Name *malcolm.*

Number

Cash *2 - 6*   Nights Booked *1*

Date *1 3 JUN 1948* **347**

SYDNEY LEE
LEADING BILLIARDS STAR
who plays for you by arrangement with
WESTERN POOLS

Autographed picture

Me, Weybourne Practice Camp, June, 1949

Regimental Running Champions
Ken Ashley (right) – 220 yards
Me – 880 yards

Customer is Wally Chapman

Standing: Charlie Hewitt, Jack Jarvis, Jim McDermott, Sgt. 'Cannonball' Conner, Sam Lodge (wearing beret) and Ernie Hartley. Kneeling: Geordie Fletcher and me. Lying down: 'Taffy' Williams.

Some of the boys – I'm 2nd left in front row. Weybourne, June 1949.

Army Form X 202/A

RELEASE LEAVE CERTIFICATE

Army No. 19179207   Present Rank... L/BDR.

Surname (Block Letters)... MacBEATH

Christian Names... ERIC Mc.BEATH

Unit, Regt. or Corps... R.A.

Date of *last entlistment...   5/6/47.

*Calling up for military service.

*Service but whichever is inapplicable.

(a) Trade on enlistment... b. Clerk   (c) Service Trade... *notice No.

(b) Trade courses and trade tests passed... *Trade Test Command Cert.   (d) Any other qualifications for civilian employment.

Military Conduct:... Very good

Testimonial: I consider that he makes a very ...

Release leave expires on ... 21 JUN 1949

Unit overseas or U.K. Stamp

2 1 JUN 1949

Officer's Signature ...

Signature of Soldier ...

Date ...

Officer i/c Unit Instruction.

(d) Record of achievement.

* Army Education Record (including particulars under (a), (b), (c) and (d) below).—
This section will not be filled in until the receipt of further War Office Instructions.

(a) Type of course.   (b) Length.   (c) Total hours of Instruction.

(i)*
(ii)*
(iii)*
(iv)*

* Entry will insert the letter "I" here to indicate that in the case of record referring to courses in which they have acted as Instructor.

Signature of Unit Education Officer ...

1. A regular soldier with ...
2. A regular soldier who ...
3. ...

THE ABOVE-NAMED PROCEEDED ON RELEASE LEAVE ON THE DATE SHOWN
IN THE MILITARY DISPERSAL UNIT STAMP OPPOSITE.

C.M.D. & D.C.U.
2 7 JUN 1949
ALDERSHOT.

N.B.—A certificate showing the date of transfer to the appropriate Army Reserve (A.F. X 202/B) will be issued by the Officer i/c Record Office.

69

Major Auret's entry in my Soldier's Release Book. No mention of Technical Assistant Course under Trade Courses.

To:- *M. E. M Malcolm*

Army Pay Office, L... (C... ... .A.),
Ci.ey lan ,
LEICESTER.

Ref:- ..B/G... ../ .ft... tl/ c/ 7122

Date:- *18. 7. 49.*

Dear Sir, Receipt of your letter dated 14.7.49 is acknowledged.
....
....
....

The final balance is arrived at as follows:-

Details of Charges and Credits.	DEBIT.			CREDIT.		
	£	s	d	£	s	d
Balance as at disposal, (27/6/49)				1	19	5
Payment at M.D.O., (27/6/49)	5	0	0			
Release Leave from 28/6/49 to 21/7/49						
.24. days Pay @ 5/- per day				6	0	0
.24. days R.A. @ 3/4 per day				4	0	0
....						
Insurance ..?. ..cks @ 2/6 per week		7	6			
....						
clothing charges fr. kit not handed in.	1	16	6			
voluntary allotment. / 22.7.49 .. 14.7.49		6	0			
Refund of clothing charges on return of kit				1	16	6
....						
Totals.	7	10	0	13	15	11
Final Balance on account. PAID {4.9.5 / 1.16.6}				6	5	11

Yours faithfully,

[signature] Eo
for it ..ontal Pymastor,
R.A.(U.A. & A.A.)

Pay Advice received after demobilization

PERIOD OF SERVICE OF MEN CALLED UP IN 1947 AND 1948.

Date of Entry.	Period of Service.		Month of Release.
1947 :	years.	months.	
January ...	2	—	1/49
February ...	2	—	2/49
March ...	2	—	3/49
April ...	2	—	4/49
May	2	—	5/49
June	2	—	6/49
July	1	11	6/49
August ...	1	11	7/49
September ...	1	10	7/49
October ...	1	9	7/49
November ...	1	9	8/49
December ...	1	8	8/49
1948 :			
January ...	1	7	8/49
February ...	1	7	9/49
March ...	1	6	9/49
April ...	1	5	9/49
May	1	5	10/49
June	1	4	10/49
July	1	3	10/49
August ...	1	3	11/49
September ...	1	2	11/49
October ...	1	1	11/49
November ...	1	1	12/49
December ...	1	—	12/49

Extract from Hansard, 18.12.1947

LOANS, LETTERS AND SUNDAYS

Thursday was payday. Many were broke by Monday or Tuesday and the usual few tried to scrounge a loan. If you gave them one, they would repay it the following Thursday, but, always believing that you had more money than they did, they would try to tap you again. My solution to this was simple and effective. At the beginning of a week, I asked the two worst offenders for a loan and, when they saw me dressing up to go out, they thought I'd been successful in acquiring one.

Letter writing sessions took place during evenings when there was no money to go out, and, as many found it extremely onerous to compose letters, I helped them. Two or three would sit at a table in the barrack room writing to my dictation while I walked up and down uttering any endearments which came to mind. And my only reward was exclamations such as, "That's great, I like that."

Sunday afternoons might have been put to the same purpose, but weren't. Newspapers, ranging from The Times to the Daily Worker, were brought in every day by a local man and, on Sunday afternoons, the gunners lay on their beds reading the Sundays. And when someone was attracted by some scandal or other in the News of the World, he would call out, "Listen to this."

It was a different story on Sunday evenings. The barrack room was deserted with most in the pubs, some in the NAAFI and others at a cinema. Although cinemas were closed in Scotland on Sundays, this was generally not the case in England and when we heard that there was a good Western being shown, four of us headed for the place where one of our number was friendly with an usherette.

On the latter's instruction, we bought tickets for the cheapest seats and the friendly usherette showed us to the front, warning us that the manager was around and adding, "I'll signal when the coast's clear, but don't all come back at once." After about five minutes, a flick of her torch indicated that the first one could go and, on saying "Excuse me" to the elderly man who occupied the aisle seat, he made his way to the dear seats. A few minutes later, the torch flashed again, the 'excuse me' made and a second gunner left. By the time the torch flashed for a third time and yet another of our party rose and said "Excuse me", the elderly gent had had enough and ordered the remaining two out.

HEALTH

Inspections of living quarters were carried out regularly. We were all naturally lazy, but some, lazier than others, reported sick for trivial reasons before morning parade. To be given light duties, such as sweeping out the barrack room or cleaning the bathhouse, was considered an achievement as much of the day could be spent relaxing on a bed.

There was an occasion, however, when the anticipated 'light duties' did not materialize although the complaint was genuine. Many, including me, had a rash around the crotch. The MO diagnosed 'laundry itch', but, after giving us ointment, he told us to 'carry on'.

The periodical FFI (Free From Infection) inspections, supervised by the MO and heartily disliked by the men, involved the entire regiment. These were to ensure that no-one had contracted any venereal disease and, although

I was never aware that anyone had, it is not something that they would be likely to broadcast.

MISDEMEANOURS

When over 2000 cigarettes were stolen from the NAAFI, we were ordered to stand by our beds while a search was carried out. On seeing a slight bulge in the front pocket of my battledress trousers, a lieutenant asked what I had there. "Something very valuable, sir," I replied and hauled out a wad of toilet paper. The search proceeded to the other huts where the culprit was easily located and arrested. He had hidden the loot in the loft of his own hut and his handprints were all over the newly whitewashed hatch.

During rifle drill, a gunner in another squad threw down his rifle and shouted, "OK, arrest me." They did and he was charged with disobeying an order and wilfully damaging Government property.

Having left the camp without permission, Gunner Eric Churchill was first posted as being AWOL and then as a deserter. He had not gone home, but to London where he approached a policeman and stated his predicament. The kindly bobby gave him money to get to a police station and give himself up, but Churchill spent the money on food before doing so. When Churchill was brought up before the CO on his return to camp, he bitterly complained that all his kit had been stolen during his absence, although, during his spell as a deserter, he had made a return trip to camp and been seen collecting it by his roommates. He was sentenced to a spell in the glasshouse.

A BIRTHDAY PARTY/GIRLS

I had taken a correspondence course at Barnard Castle, but, as evening classes were available on the doorstep in Gravesend, I attended an art class in the summer and English, shorthand and typing classes during the winter. Almost all the students were girls and when a girl in the typing class invited me to a friend's birthday party and said to bring some pals, I asked, "How many?"

"Could you manage seven? she replied.

On selecting the required number, I asked them to contribute towards a present for the girl. They willingly did so and I bought a brooch in the figure of a swallow.

On the evening of the party, the address which the girl had given me proved difficult to locate, but we eventually found it, near the river and next door to a pub. In response to my loud knocking, our hostess ushered us in and we found ourselves in a fair sized hall, decorated with balloons and streamers. There were many other girls and blokes of our own age present, and, like them, we were smartly dressed in civvies so that we didn't stand out.

When an older man entered by a side door, the girl introduced him as her father. "Have a good time, boys," he said, "There's plenty to drink. Just go through and ask at the bar." The side door led directly into the pub and Dad was the landlord.

With a small band providing music for dancing and with a good supply of grub, we had a most enjoyable evening. And, as I was teetotal and the others somewhat abstemious in their consumption of alcohol, nobody over indulged.

The present, too, proved a winner and the girl laughed when she opened the box. "It's very appropriate," she said. "Why?" I asked.

"My name's Bird," she replied.

I met a student nurse at another party and took her out several times before a friend of hers informed me that, since meeting me, she had ceased to study for her exams. On learning this, and as I had no wish for a long relationship, I advised the girl to concentrate on her nursing studies and stopped seeing her.

MAJOR GRUBB

My first meeting with Major Grubb was when he entered the Control Room with Lieutenant Hickey. As the NCO in charge, I drew the others to attention and he gave us a mere cursory glance before surveying the place, with the lieutenant explaining the layout. Grubb, who up till then had remained silent, suddenly pounced on a telephone and, holding it base up, commanded, "Get a screwdriver." A gunner brought the tool. "Open it," ordered Grubb and then, when it was open, "Look," he barked, "corrosion. This is a serious fault. A Command Post is no use without an efficient communications system."

Major Grubb had come from a signals' battery at Barnard Castle, and his performance in the Control Room suggested to us that he knew little or nothing of Heavy Ack Ack equipment as, with thousands of pounds worth of the stuff around him, he had chosen to examine a telephone! And as he had berated Hickey in front of us, it also told us that he was no gentleman. Nevertheless, after he had inspected the Control Room on a subsequent occasion, he turned to me and said, "Very good, Bombardier Malcolm. Thank you."

JANKERS AND ALMOST JANKERS

I was ordered to drill a defaulter. It was a warm afternoon, the man was loaded up with full marching equipment and we were in full view of the RSM's office. When we were some distance away, I gave the perspiring gunner a break by calling him to a halt and pretending to tighten his straps. But, as we were aware that the RSM was watching from his window, I called, "ATTENTION, SHOULDER ARMS, QUICK MARCH, LEFT, RIGHT." And, when the figure at the window disappeared, "HALT AND STAND EASY". With the defaulter and me working as a team, this pattern obtained throughout the punishment as, similar to most, conscripted, junior, NCOs, I had sympathy for those who merely *bent* the rules.

Our hut had just passed an inspection, and we were pleased with ourselves, when in stormed Lt. Hickey. "You're on a charge, Bombardier," he screeched at me, "You disobeyed my order." I didn't know what he was talking about, but he soon informed me. "I told you yesterday to be in the gun park at 1430 hours today and (raising his voice) **you were not there**." I remained silent, but he was right. I had forgotten. "What are you gonna do, Bomb?" asked a sympathetic gunner after Hickey had left. To which I truthfully replied, "No idea."

Two days later, I was relieved of my cap and belt and marched into the Battery Commander's room between two NCOs. The Major was seated at his desk, with Hickey standing at his side and the charge of 'disobeying an order' was read out. "Have you anything to say?" asked the Major.

"I admit to being guilty as charged, sir," I replied, "but I cannot be in two places at the same time."

"What do you mean, Bombardier?" asked the Major.

"Well, sir, I obeyed the last order I was given," I replied.

"What order was that? he asked.

"Battery orders, on the notice board, instructed us to be in the huts for a room inspection at 1415 hours," I explained. The Major turned to Hickey, who remained silent, and then, looking at me, said "When you're given a verbal order you must make a note of it in future. Case dismissed on this occasion."

Outside the room, my escort slapped me on the back and there was rejoicing in the barrack room that night!

MY FRIEND, THE RSM

It is likely that the RSM had detected slackness within the regiment as he posted a notice ordering all bombardiers to attend a two-week course which he, personally, would conduct. Every day began with a thorough inspection followed by a drilling session when gunners, taking care that the RSM didn't see them, smirked as they passed. During one of his lectures, he stated that there were seven types of men in the British Army; two of which he defined as follows: "Bdr. Dye is one who will carry out an order to the letter. Then there's Bdr. Malcolm. (I waited with baited breath.) Give him a pen, paper and books and he's happy." "Not bad," I thought, and although I had had virtually no contact with the man, this made me realize that he had correctly assessed the character of those under his command. What the RSM didn't know, however, was that my pal L/Bdr Bob Shield and I had every intention of missing the second week of his course as we had been accepted for a two-week course of study at Nottingham University's Lenton Hurst Residential College, organized by the Regional Committee for Adult Education in HM Forces.

As we needed the RSM's permission to go, Bob felt that we should tell him right away. But, fearing that he might be more liable to refuse if given time to consider, I said to wait until the end of the week when it would be too late to stop us. And so, after a hard week, consisting mainly of marching and rifle drill, we sprung our surprise on the RSM; emphasizing that it was an educational course. The latter consideration seemed to do the trick and he raised no objection whatever.

Some time after my studies at Lenton Hurst College, I received an admission card to the Civil Service Examinations being held in the Hotel Victoria, Northumberland Avenue, London, SW1. I sat the three-hour papers in English, Mathematics, Geography and French and the two-hour paper in General Knowledge. And, months later, learned that I had failed only Maths and French – not bad considering the little study I put in. As far as I was concerned, the whole exercise was mainly to escape the boredom of Army routine and in this I had been wholly successful. But I was yet to learn of the importance of these exams to the regular soldier.

I was Guard Commander and everything was running smoothly with the guard at the gate and the others listening to the wireless in the guardroom. But, on returning to the latter after a trip to the Battery Office, I found the wireless switched off because the RSM had ordered it. Ten minutes later I put the wireless on again, low, and we were enjoying the music when a clerk appeared saying, "Bombardier, the RSM wants to see you." And, fearing that I had overstepped the mark, I reported at his office, only two doors away.

After some hesitation, the RSM said, "Bombardier, (my mouth was quite dry by now) I have a problem and you may be able to help me." (Was he being sarcastic?) "You have some knowledge of the Civil Service Exams (I relaxed) and I'd like you to tell me if I'm studying the right things." He then went on to explain that, without certificates, he could be demoted so that I gave him guidance regarding the subjects I was best at, but advised him to consult another bombardier concerning mathematics.

Enquiring heads were raised on my return to the guardroom and "What did he say?" was eagerly asked. "He said he was enjoying the music and asked why it had been switched off," I joked as I walked over to the wireless and turned it on. "Come off it," said a gunner. "Well, I can't tell you what he said, but I'll tell you this. He and I are mates." Then as I saw the RSM leave his office, I called out, "Turn the volume up a bit." We could now relax, as the Orderly Officer wouldn't be round until midnight. But I now knew why the RSM had so willingly allowed us to go to Lenton Hurst College. We had been used as guinea pigs and this man, who had been through the War, was now fearful of examinations.

CROSBY

MPs (Military Policemen) are professional policemen who do not have to live with those they arrest. RPs (Regimental Policemen), on the other hand, are appointed by their own superiors and, as they *have* to live with those they arrest, prefer to avoid taking such action. Therefore none of us wanted RP duty; usually given to junior NCOs.

Together with another NCO, I was on RP duty one Saturday night in Gravesend. We had patrolled through the town, then down by the River Thames, before deciding to visit a dancehall which we, ourselves, frequented. On being allowed free admittance, we saw that the hall was packed and regretted that we could not participate in the dance. As we were so hot in our uniform greatcoats, we were about to leave when a disturbance broke out in the crowd. The bouncers moved in and pulled a soldier towards us whom we immediately recognized as Crosby. Apparently, he had not caused any trouble, but the manager asked us to take him away as he was drunk and becoming loud mouthed.

The fresh air didn't rouse Crosby and, without our assistance, he would never have managed back to barracks and, now after midnight, all he wanted to do was sleep. It was with difficulty that we kept him awake and, having marched him past the sentry by the guardhouse, we entered his hut in the dark, dropped him on an empty bed and threw a blanket over him.

After breakfast next morning, I went to see if Crosby had sobered up and found the bed empty. "Where's Crosby?" I asked.
"He's gone," was the reply.

"What do you mean *gone?*" I asked.

"He woke up at 8 o'clock and couldn't think how he got here. He cursed that he would be late for cookhouse duty and dashed off."

I could only smile. "He wouldn't be much late," I replied.

"He would, you know. He doesn't belong here now. He was posted to Bostal Heath two weeks ago."

McDERMOTT

Gunner Jim McDermott often entertained us by brilliantly mimicking the peculiar high-pitched voice of Lieutenant Hickey, but there was one occasion when this could have led to trouble. Hickey, who issued orders from the Control Room by tannoy to the gun crews outside, had gone to the Battery Office and I was left in charge. "Let's keep the gun crews busy," suggested McDermott and we then went through practice runs of preparing to fire with each man shouting "Steady" when the instrument needles finally settled. McDermott was in his element at the tannoy screeching 'FIRE' in Hickey's voice until our spy outside gave warning that the officer was returning. And as the gun crews did not notice Hickey returning, they were unaware that they had been kept unnecessarily busy which would have no doubt incurred their wrath.

Sam Lodge and I were detailed to whitewash the ceiling of the Control Room, on 17 June, 1948, but after we had spent a whole day trying to get the necessary materials, but had succeeded in finding only the whitewash and one 1" brush, Major Grubb cancelled the operation anyway. Typically, however, the order to whitewash came again a week later and this time with Jim McDermott as my assistant, all the materials were procured, including sheets to cover the equipment.

"This job's going to take us a week," I remarked.
"They paint hundreds of cars in that time at Ford's in Dagenham," replied Jim.
"True," I said, "but they use spray guns."

As we looked at each other, I could see that our minds were channelling in the same direction.
The only sprays at our disposal were stirrup pumps and within half-an-hour we had procured a pump and a bucket of whitewash. "I'll do the pumping and you hold the spray," I said, and, as I agreed to swop places at a later stage, he raised no objection. With a foot firmly placed on the footrest of the stirrup pump, I crouched over the bucket while McDermott pointed the spray nozzle at the part of ceiling directly above his head. "Right," I shouted, and began pumping like mad. Not only did the spray hit the ceiling, but it cascaded over McDermott and there was whitewash everywhere.

Fortunately, we had almost succeeded in cleaning the place when Hickey came in. "Clear it up," he ordered, "and get on with the job." But there was no *dampening* of McDermott's spirit as, when Hickey had gone, his comment was "We'll use a finer spray next time and it's your turn to hold it."

A COSTLY REPLY

One sunny day, when my squad was on the parade ground, the BSM appeared and decided to inspect us. We stood at attention looking straight ahead as, walking slowly up and down the lines, he looked over each man from top to bottom. Eventually, he arrived in front on me and, first, addressing the whole squad said, "A shambles." And then, to me, "Bombardier, your boots." I looked at my clean boots.

"Now look at mine." I looked at his.

"See the difference?" he asked. And when I said nothing, he went on, "The difference is mine has a shine and yours doesn't."

It was perhaps due the familiarity bred from having been in his office that I then spoke up. "There is a difference, sir," I agreed. "The difference is that you have a batman and I don't."

If looks could kill, I was dead, but he said nothing and strode off. But the squad knew that I had damned the lot of us and this was confirmed when all weekend leave passes were cancelled before evening.

I was in the gun park over three weeks later when a messenger arrived to tell me that the BSM wanted to see me. This made the squad surmise that further retribution was in the offing, but I found the man in a relaxed mood and he asked, "Well, have you learned your lesson?"

"Yes, sir, I have," I replied, "but it hasn't been a fair lesson."

"Why is that? he asked.

"Well," I said, "Londoners can visit their homes as they are only a short distance away, but others can't."

His reaction to this surprised me. "How would you like to go to a show tonight?"

On returning to the gun park with a glum face, the others, fearing the worst, asked what had transpired. Pointing to each one of the group in turn, I said, "You, you, you…You're going to a show in London tonight." Despair turned to elation and the BSM would have been proud of the speed at which we all got ready and set off for London with spit and polished boots.

LONDON

Servicemen often headed for the Nuffield Centre where dances were held and where free tickets to the not so popular stage shows were easily obtained. I got a ticket for 'Lute Song', at the Winter Garden Theatre in Drury Lane, in which Yul Brynner was a principal and Millicent Martin had small parts. And, although the show eventually failed, I liked it. Perhaps the reason it failed was that it was a sad story of famine in China and, with the War, with its deprivations, so recently behind us, the public were looking for something more cheerful. I also went to see the popular review 'Sugar And Spice' in which Bill Owen (Compo in the TV series 'Last of the Summer Wine') and Ethel Revnell starred. When the audience roared with laughter at one of Owen's suggestive jokes, the girl in front of me asked her sailor boy friend, "What does he mean?" but the latter fudged his reply.

Normally, we went to the dancing in Gravesend or Dartford, but, on the odd occasion, to the Hammersmith Palais. This was the era of the big bands and, at the

Hammersmith, we danced to those of Lou Preager and Joe Loss.

I was still in touch with Jim Wilson, my boyhood pal, who was now a corporal drill instructor at Yeovil in Somerset. We met, by arrangement, in London, booked overnight accommodation at the Union Jack Club in Waterloo Road and headed off to the Hammersmith Palais.

The first question usually asked by a dancing partner was "Do you come here often?" while the second one was "Where do you come from?" When my partner asked the second question and I replied, "Dundee", she said, "Oh, I've just been dancing with another Scotsman, but he's from Edinburgh." A moment or two later, she pointed out Jim and I was not surprised. He was behaving true to form.

Jim returned late to the Club and explained this the following morning. He had seen a girl home and, as she lived a good distance away, they had taken the Tube. But he had walked all
the way back. I, on the other hand, had had a good night's sleep.

(On being demobbed, Jim brought a Yeovil girl back with him to Dundee where she shared a bedroom with his sister, Margaret, before finding other accommodation and a job in the box office of the Repertory Theatre. Jim then decided to emigrate to Canada, as his brother, Walter, had already done. The Yeovil girl was left in Dundee and he married a Canadian.)

A weekend stay in London was made courtesy of Bob Shield's uncle who allowed Bob to use a flat he owned.

Bob's uncle, a caterer who managed Noel Coward's functions, left the key at a nearby pub and we collected it from there.

On the one and only occasion I went with a few others to the Locarno Ballroom at Streatham Hill, we stood no chance with the girls as the place was teeming with American soldiers and we were in civvies.

Lyon's Corner Houses were popular with the public as they provided good food at reasonable prices. And, when we were given seventy-two-hour passes, I think it was Eric Churchill who suggested trying for a job at one of them. "Doing what?" he was asked. "Anything they ask you to," he replied. It was, of course, against Army Regulations to take on a second job, but, with the object of taking one, Bob Shield, Sam Lodge, Eric Churchill and I hitched a lift to London on the evening of Friday, 11 June, 1948 and booked into The Salvation Army Red Shield Hostel, St James' Park, at 2/6d (12½p) a night.

At about 7.45am on Saturday, Churchill led the expedition to a back door of Lyon's Piccadilly Corner House where we joined a small queue before being hired and then shown into an upstairs, stone-floored, room containing machinery. Now, if a soldier is put on 'jankers', he is likely to find himself peeling spuds in the cookhouse, but, although we hadn't expected to be doing this kind of thing in Lyon's, this was different as we were being paid at the handsome rate of 1/8d (approx. 8p) an hour. It wasn't all that bad, however, as machines cleaned the potatoes and we had only to take the eyes out. And, in addition to our remuneration, we were provided with lunch, afternoon snacks and high tea in the staff canteen. At the end of the shift, we swilled out and brushed the floor before standing around waiting for our pay and a pass for meal at 5.30pm. However, on Monday, the last day of our three-day stint, the routine changed for me as I was given the job of hauling bins of prepared potatoes through the cake-decorating floor to an elevator. All in all, we rather enjoyed the whole business and especially the change from Army cooking. But there was the additional pleasure of having earned a total of £1.19s.2d. (about £1.96p).

FOOD

On Saturday afternoons and occasionally in the evenings, we patronized the small café just outside Milton Barracks where the meals were good and reasonably priced. On returning from a sojourn at Bostal Heath, we found the café under new ownership and the proprietor, eager to please his customers, enquired if we had enjoyed our meal. And, when we said that the chips weren't brown enough, he remedied the complaint.

The Army, however, did not take the same interest in our taste buds and operated on the principle of 'If it's edible, eat it'. The question, "Did you enjoy your meal?", was, therefore, never asked and, if it had been, it's a certainty that a number of facetious gunners would have called out "No". Towards the end of every meal, the question put by the orderly officer was "Any complaints?" when the only dissenting voice would generally be that of a wit, *after* the officer had gone.

This, however, was not always the case. "There's hairs in this mince, sir" is received with astonishment by a junior officer who is compelled to peer into the small portion left on the plate while the others at the table assume serious looks. It's the gunner's own hair and, although the officer suspects this, he cannot say so. He takes up the plate, heads in the direction of the cookhouse and returns shortly saying that he hopes that such a thing will not occur again. But, like all of us, he knows full well that it will and, being a wise young man, he has not spoken to the cookhouse staff.

Lance Bombardier Dye complained that his two slices of bread were under the minimum weight ration. A weighing machine was brought to the table and, to his delight and that of his companions, he was proved correct – but only by a whisker! (Bread had not been rationed during the war, but was rationed between July, 1946 and July, 1948.)

I awakened on Christmas morning, to find a mug of tea and a mince pie by the side of my bed. Normally, we waited in line to receive our food from the cookhouse staff, but, on Christmas Day, Officers and senior NCOs served us at tables. As Christmas meals are excellent, complaints are almost unknown, but, although it was not made to an officer, I had one when I was on RP duty on Christmas Day, 1948.

Along with those of the guard, my dinner was brought to the guard house by the cooks and, as the helpings were insufficient, I shared out mine among the others and went to, what was by then, an empty dining room. A sergeant cook appeared and, when I voiced my complaint, he told me to sit down. Within ten minutes, he presented me with a meal fit for royalty and, while I tucked in, he regaled me with stories of his time in the North African desert where he had cooked on an outdoor stove. That sergeant cook made my Christmas Day duty a memorable one, but I made no mention of my feast to the others.

The padre was kind enough to invite me to tea that day, but, being on RP duty, I had to decline.

SPORTS

There was great rivalry between the three batteries and Ken Ashley, in our battery, had already won the 100 yards race when another gunner and I were preparing to run the mile.

Knowing that a particularly good runner in another battery was participating, my partner said to me, "We haven't a hope."
"We have two advantages," I replied.
"Such as?" he asked.
"Well, he's already been in a race." said I.
"So what?" replied my partner. "He won, didn't he?"
"Yes, he did, so maybe he's tired now," I replied.
"No chance," said my despondent partner, "but what's the second advantage?"
"You," I said, and announced my plan. "Three quarters way round the first lap, you will force a fast pace from the others by bursting ahead while I stay back to conserve my energy."

At the selected point, my partner took off like a hare and, taking the bait, all the others increased their pace to keep up with him; all, that is, except our main adversary who remained beside me. A short distance into the second circuit, my running mate slipped on the grass and, lying exhausted, gave me a weak wave of support as I passed.

Those in front were tiring and, when I overtook them, the members of my battery were yelling their heads off. I didn't look back and, as I burst through the tape, my legs collapsed under me. We had won by our joint effort! But I was in such a state of exhaustion that I had to be helped to pull my trousers on, over my shorts.

I took part in an event where two teams, of seven men, competed to pull a large coir match into their respective areas. The men stood on opposite sides of the mat and darted for its attached loops at the sound of a whistle. And, with 'Geordie' Fletcher, a powerful P.T. instructor in our team, we brought the mat over our line, after a struggle. But we now had the next team to face and, as it was stronger, I suggested a plan of action.

Hitting was not permitted, but, as soon as the whistle was blown, five of us held hands and dashed across the mat to obstruct the passage of the opposing team. Taken by surprise, they were brought to a halt while our other two members grasped the loops and hauled the mat over our line! Such a tactic could be used only once, of course, and, in the final, we were so evenly matched against our opponents, that, after a twenty-minute melee and much to the relief of both drained teams, a draw was declared. On another occasion, I participated in an equally rough game of shinty during which I collected the scar which I still bear.

Football was my preferred sport, but when I was selected for the First Eleven, I withdrew because my father, accompanied by a friend, chose that particular Saturday to visit me. Although I did get a game at a later date, a permanent position was denied me as many players were of professional standard.

Coming more under the heading of entertainment, we were treated, one evening, to a snooker exhibition by the professional, Sydney Lee. A Welsh gunner was very good indeed, but Lee beat him easily.

TRAIN JOURNEYS

Trains were still usually crowded in post-war Britain and, on a north-bound train, I gave up my precious seat to a middle-aged lady who readily accepted it. But, although this left me standing in the corridor for hours, she never thought of letting me have the seat for a spell. On another occasion, when travelling overnight, I had a good night's sleep on my greatcoat in a crammed corridor. If, by some miracle, a train was not full, I preferred it to be of the compartment type and not the Pullman, as you could stretch out on the seats and pull down the corridor blind. But I never went the length of writing JUST MARRIED on the window, as some soldiers did.

As soon as a train stopped at a station, people would dive on to the platform to purchase tea and food from platform trolleys. An RAF chap left it a bit late and I watched him gingerly carrying two mugs of tea as the train began to leave. And when willingly hands yanked him on board and half the contents were spilt, he was in no way grateful.

On a train from Dundee, I met John Coates; an acquaintance of mine who was in the RAF and stationed at Hornchurch. John informed me that he had recently been on a course in religious education where the food and accommodation had been good, but from which, judging by the oaths he used, he had not drawn a great deal of benefit. This, however, put the idea in my mind and I decided to ask the BSM's permission when I arrived back in Milton Barracks.

I was on my way to the BSM's office when I changed my mind about the type of course. "I can see you're busy, sir," I began, "but I won't take up much of your time."

"Well?" he asked.

"I'd like to be able to drive, sir, and would be more useful to the Army if I could attend a 15-cwt Truck Drivers' Course."

Sitting at his desk, he raised a hand to support his chin before replying in a somewhat weary fashion. "Others come into the Army to train as soldiers and perhaps do a course. "You spend your time on courses and do some soldiering in between them. The answer is NO."

BAD NEWS

The regiment was drawn up on the parade ground and the morning sky appropriately overcast when the CO announced that the period to be served by National Servicemen had been extended by up to three months. Audible groans greeted this dismal news and few paid any attention to the rest of the speech which ended, "and I expect every soldier to perform his duties as enthusiastically as he has done in the past."

Many of the *enthusiastic* gunners kept tabs on the number of days to their release so that, back in the barrack room, fresh calculations were made. "That makes 265 days for me," said one.

"386 for me," said another. And so it went on; sometimes interspersed by "And don't forget the breakfast" or other such witticisms.

MISERABLE SOLDIERS

A gunner, posted into the battery, was given accommodation in the hut next to mine. I went across to see him in the evening and was surprised to find him in an otherwise deserted room; a forlorn figure, sitting on his bed. After some conversation he soon perked up and although only eighteen, he was married. Understanding his feeling of loneliness, I told him to come and have a chat with me at any time.

Some men didn't take to service life at all and, on more than one occasion, I witnessed a well-spoken, and obviously a well-off, gunner trying to escape by drinking spirits. Sitting by himself at a table, he never used the same glass twice, but attempted to cover the table with his empties. Yet I never saw him laid low. The foregoing, however, did not apply to Bombardier Ebo whose stag party we joyfully attended.

FLOOD DUTY

Although the Thames floods of 1948 were nothing as serious as those of March, 1947, they were serious enough for farmers whose fields were inundated. The Army was called upon and we worked hard in the Gillingham area; heaving sand-filled jute bags into positions to form a barrier to the water.

When I tasted my tea during the evening meal, I didn't like it at all. It had been laced with rum and, on returning it to the serving counter, a young subaltern said that everyone had to take the rum. "I will do," I replied, "but not in my tea." As the officer accepted this apparent compromise, I collected a neat rum and returned to my table where it was readily consumed by another soldier.

THE TATTOO

Milton Barracks was a hive of activity preparing for the three-day GRAND MILITARY TATTOO AND EXHIBITION of July/August, 1948. The official programme outlined the history of THE ROYAL REGIMENT OF ARTILLERY, the objects of THE ROYAL ARTILLERY ASSOCIATION and the OTHER ATTRACTIONS. The main attraction was, of course, the TATTOO, while the EXHIBITION included a Japanese suicide plane, German V1 and V2 'buzz' bombs, 40mm Bofors LAA guns, a 25-pounder field gun, an HAA 3.7 gun, a radar room and a barrack room.

LANGHAM CAMP, NEAR STIFFKEY

When the regiment was going to Langham Camp, I travelled there in the advance party on 6 August to prepare for the arrival of the regiment. It duly arrived on the 10th and during our stay, we marched the 1½ miles to the firing camp in Stiffkey where I renewed my acquaintance with Captain Dick and Sgt. Major Butchard. Radar and visual (tracker) methods were employed to aim the guns and the latter two men supervised the operations.

We returned to Milton Barracks on the 31st. Reveille was at 0500, the special train left Wells-on-Sea at 0700 and we were *home* by 1700.

We always paraded in the morning, but, the following day, the BSM called a second parade at 1430. He was displeased with the state of the rooms and encouraged the NCOs to put those responsible on a charge.

BOSTAL HEATH

On Thursday, 2 September, 1948, my 48-hour pass was cancelled because we were going to Bostal Heath to have what was referred to as a Battle of Britain exercise. We went in trucks and, as it was a short journey, I went into Welling for afternoon tea before going to the pictures. That, however, proved to be the only relaxation I was to have as Hickie then had us on a 6 hours on and six hours off rota. On duty, we did nothing but plot targets in various forms while, off duty, I either slept or ate cakes. However, something must have gone wrong on the Sunday night, as, out of the blue, the order STAND DOWN was given at 4am and we, thankfully, went to bed. On Monday, we returned to Gravesend.

The following March, there was talk of the regiment moving to Cyprus and that embarkation leave was a certainty, but, when we did move, it was only for another spell at Bostal Heath.

Denning, the self-professed idiot whom I referred to earlier, had become something of a pal of mine. He was up to his usual tricks and at a very early hour of the day that Advance Party was to leave for Bostal, he was in the guardhouse when Lt. Ford entered. "There's been a fire in the camp, sir," said Denning

"Where? Where? asked the alarmed Lieutenant.

"April fool, sir," replied Denning with a smile; whereupon, the relieved officer managed a sickly one in return.

Denning, who had a girlfriend in the NAAFI to supply him with cigarettes and cakes, had, a couple of weeks earlier, gone home on a weekend pass, but, having got an obliging doctor to provide him with a sickness note, he returned a week later.

I was in the Advance Party which travelled to Bostal Heath on Friday, 1 April and the main party, including practically the whole of 37 Battery, arrived on Monday. Sgt. 'Cannonball' Connor, who arrived on Tuesday, had been very crafty in choosing a decent gun crew while leaving Sgt. Goodchild with all the crackpots, including Denning. I shared a hut with my pal Bob Shield, and Jack Jarvis obligingly rigged up a bed lamp for me. Bob, however, was moved and Ted Richardson shared with me. And, whereas Bob was extremely untidy, Ted was the opposite; even going to the length of stuffing ply wood into his pack to keep it square.

It was well after midnight when I left the warm guardroom to check on the sentry at the gate. The huts were some distance away and, when I saw a light come on in one of them, I told two gunners to come with me to investigate.

The door of the hut was wide open and smoke was pouring out. The occupants were awake and, after we had rushed around opening all the windows to clear the air, one told me that he had had difficult in finding the light switch due to the smoke. It didn't take long to find the cause of the fire as Brady's trousers lay smouldering on the floor beside his bed. He had fallen asleep when smoking in bed and I told him his carelessness could have had serious consequences. To the best of my knowledge, neither he, nor anyone else, carried out this dangerous practice again and the incident cost him a replacement pair of trousers.

Jack Jarvis and I decided to go into the hairdressing business. There was only the small village of Abbey Wood within walking distance and Woolwich and Welling were some distance away so that it wasn't easy to get to a barbershop. And, to increase our monopoly, I took advantage of my exalted rank by making liberal use of the order 'GET YOUR HAIR CUT'. We started off with only one pair of scissors between us, and no clippers. The charge was 6d (2½p), but when a chap wanted his hair thinned out, something I had never previously done, it cost him a bob (1/-/5p). And when some fellows asked if I had cut hair before, I truthfully said, "Yes" without mentioning this was only my almost bald grandfather's! Then we struck lucky as a chap presented us with a pair of non-electric clippers while another lent us a similar pair; both on the understanding that they got free haircuts.

Athletic pursuits were always encouraged and I was in charge of the group of runners which passed the guardhouse, turned right along the road then, as soon as we were out of sight of the camp, swung left into the woods. It was a warm afternoon and we were soon stretched out in the shade beside a small stream in which to cool our feet. After a couple of hours lazing about in this paradise, I said, "Time to go" and damped my face, armpits and both sides of my vest to give the appearance of sweating. Seeing me do this, the others began splashing so much water around that I had to tell them not to overdo it. We entered the camp at great speed and a 2nd Lieutenant confronted me at the huts. "Had a good run?" he enquired. The others were all gasping for breath or doubled up with pain as I panted, "Yes, sir."

A group of us commandeered a three-ton lorry to attend a dance on a Saturday night. The lorry was driven by Gunner Churchill and, on the return journey, Gunner Williams was beside him in the cab and the rest of us in the back. Driving along a country lane, Churchill began to act the fool by first careering from side to side on the road and then driving up and down the grass verges. And, while sounds of enjoyment were heard issuing from the cab, we at the back lost our holds and began slithering about on the metal floor. Jim McDermott suffered an arm injury, others had their shoulders hurt, and, when the nightmare journey was over, I jumped out, opened the cab door, and yanked Churchill out. Churchill flicked off his army belt and threatened me with it. But I was extremely angry and when, with the others standing around, I warned him of the consequences and said I would wrap it round his neck, he backed down. A good night had been spoiled by Churchill's foolishness; the result of him having had one too many at the dance.

We sometimes went to the dancehall in Welling where Bob Shield acquired one girlfriend and I acquired two!

When we first arrived at Bostal Heath, 2nd Lt. Chessun came up to me and said, "I'm in charge of the Control Room during the training here. You'll be instructing, Bombardier."

"Instructing, sir?"

"Yes, on the equipment," he answered; rather surprised.

"Oh, you know, sir, I don't feel I'm qualified to instruct now. I've done very little in the past year."

Chessun thought for a bit while I blew my nose. "Well," he said, "I'm newly off a course and you'll only be helping me until Bdr. Webb comes back from his course. You could look at your drill book in the evenings after I've told you what we'll be on the following day."

It was now my turn to think a bit before I said, "All right, sir," - without any intension of consulting any book.

Chessun's first lecture, 'An Introduction to Equipment', was anything but interesting to Jack Jarvis, Sam Lodge (both Tech. Acks.), Jim McDermott, Taffy Williams, Ernie Hewitt, Ernie Hartley and myself – all in 111 Group and nearing demob. So much so that Hartley, with hands in pockets, kept muttering, "Only ten weeks to go" and "Roll on demob."

Against regulations, I saw a testimonial which Lt. Ford wrote about me and, as I did not care much for him, I was surprised at its contents: AN INTELLIGENT NCO WHO HAS A GOOD APPEARANCE AND IS CAPABLE. WILL WORK WELL WHEN NOT SUPERVISED AND CAN INSTRUCT SATIFACTORILY. AN ASSET TO HIS FUTURE EMPLOYER. (I quoted this in a letter home and added "Who wouldn't be at 30/- (£1.50p) a week?" – my wage in the office.

ARMY COLLEGE (NORTH)/WELBECK ABBEY

When I learned that, prior to demob, service men and women could attend Army College (North), at Welbeck Abbey near Worksop, I eagerly applied and was accepted.

I arrived at Welbeck on 25 April, 1949 and was immediately impressed by the place as the College was an imposing mansion, standing in spacious grounds. There were football and rugby pitches, a bowling green, a cinema, a library, a games room, a billiard room, a YMCA, a main NAAFI, a sub NAAFI (in the *Abbey) a barber shop and an information bureau. And on the evening of my arrival, I attended a 'Get Together Dance' for O.Rs. (Other Ranks) in the underground ballroom which contained so many paintings that it looked more like an art gallery. What a place to study. *The recorded history of the Abbey begins in 1154, but little of the original building remained.

Most of the students were billeted in Nissen huts and I was placed in Hut No. 6 with eleven others. We were all studying different subjects – English, Foreign Languages, Physics, Biology, Mathematics, Commercial Subjects, History, Geography, Psychology, Philosophy, Trade Subjects of all descriptions, etc. - and there were so many of us that there were two meal sittings. There were also some ATS girls; one studying music and the others, shorthand and typing. During evenings in the NAAFI, I would see a group sitting with Pitman's books.

Most of the students were well-educated, decent types, and I found a particular pal in Carlos Rabeiro whose home was in Glasgow. Carlos spoke with a slight Glasgow accent and, although proficient in Portuguese, Spanish and French, he had chosen the latter two as his study subjects.

Lectures ran from 0900 until 1800, but, as our individual lectures did not run concurrently, the remainder of the time was given to private study. Most evenings, there was an optional, but well attended, lecture beginning at 1800; on such subjects as 'The Nature of Philosophy', 'The

Human Brain, 'Straight and Crooked Thinking', 'Why Study History', 'What use is Education?', 'Law and Order in the Middle Ages' and the 'History of Welbeck Abbey'. There also a Mock Parliament, gramophone recitals, plays, modern poetry and whist drives.

My course was in the Modern Studies Department and, in the morning, I had the choice of attending either the Geography lecture, given by Sgt. James of the RAEC, or the English one given by Mr R. Venables. At the start, I went to the Geography class, but, when I heard that Mr Venables was more entertaining, I switched to English. English became a popular subject because Mr Venables, who wore a black gown ripped to shreds at the bottom, read risqué passages from good literature. Obviously, he knew his audience and was encouraging them to read the old masters.

As the course was so good, plus the fact that I had a girlfriend in *Creswell, and Worksop was near at hand with its cinemas and dancehall, I was enjoying myself so much that I applied for an extension. Dr Grout was Head of the Modern Studies Department and, on learning from him that my application had been refused, I went to his office to find out why. But, as the secretary was unable to provide the answer, I 'phoned my Battery Commander at Gravesend; reversing the charges. *In a letter to my brother, I described Creswell as having only about half-a-dozen houses, one picture house, which was packed five minutes after opening and the only one in England closed on Sundays, and twenty to thirty chip shops. All a *slight* exaggeration.

Major Grubb, who had actually shaken hands with me before he left, had been replaced by Major Auret and, when I asked him to reconsider his decision, he said, "Well, Malcolm, I gave this much consideration before, but have decided you're required at firing camp. However, I've seen the Education Department and they say you can go to Welbeck again after the camp."

"But I'm being demobbed on the 27th of next month," I responded.

"You can be demobbed later," he replied.

This, of course, would mean that I would be on the extension course during my demob leave, but, not wanting to let him think that I was interested in attending the College only in the Army's time, I kept quiet.

"You can arrange it with your instructor," said the Major, "and I'll see that it's all right at this end."

I asked my mathematics lecturer if I could go into the advanced class if I continued. "You're already in it," was his surprising answer, "but, if you wish, I'll give you private tutorials." However, when Dr. Grout informed me that nobody was allowed to go on these courses during their demob leave, I again 'phoned Major Auret, reversing the charges, to tell him this, but he remained adamant.

On returning to Gravesend, I was in the company of Charlie Hewitt, who had done a trade course at Welbeck, when we met the Major. A very different officer from Major Grubb, he asked how we had got on and apologised to me for his refusal. Then, with a broad smile, he added, "I know what Welbeck's like and know why you wanted to stay on."

A DECEPTION AND A NEAR THING

After our chat with Major Auret, we went to see BSM Hill who tried his best to look sympathetic as he said to me, "Sorry you didn't get your extension, Bombardier."

"Yes, it was hard luck, wasn't it?" I replied. "Well, what about a spot of leave now?"

"Nobody's getting leave till 14 July," said Hill.

"But I'm being demobbed on 27 June. Can I get it with my demob leave?"

This was, of course, ridiculous so that he didn't know what to say other than "Oh, I don't know about that." And then to Hewitt, "You'll be going to Bostal Heath" and to me "You can go on the police staff."

"Can't I go to Bostal too?" I asked.

"No," he replied, "There are already four NCOs at Bostal. By the way, the Major wants to ask a favour of you 111 Group fellows. Would you stop in the Army another week because we need you for a certain exercise at Bostal Heath immediately after firing camp?

"Hey," I objected, "We get demobbed on the very last day of our group."

"What do you say, Hewitt?"

"Well, it's only another week. Yes," said Charlie.

Then, to me, "And what about you, Bombardier?"

Not wanting to offend Hill altogether, I replied that I'd give it some thought although, in my mind the answer was, "Nothing doing, mate."

After this meeting with us, Hill told the other fellows that Charlie and I had *both* volunteered to stay on another week. The result of this deception was that all, except one, agreed to stay on. But, when I put them straight on the issue, one by one and including Charlie, went to Hill's office and told him they'd changed their minds. Hartley was the last to renege and Hill was so wild that he said to him, "Righto, I'll detail you." – a threat that was impossible to carry out. In any case, neither Charlie nor I got any particular job and, with the rest of the battery at either a big rally at the Albert Hall or at Woolwich practising for it, we, together with Jack Jarvis and another bloke, had practically the whole week off.

It was, however, a near thing for Charlie and me. There was only a skeleton staff in the barracks and the BSM said to me, "A man has had to call off in London. Go and put on your best uniform and report back to me." But, not wanting to go, I deliberately exposed the worn lapels of my Canadian battledress before returning to the office. The keen eyes of the BSM immediately focused on the lapels and, with barely a moment's hesitation, he said, "Tell Hewitt to put on his best uniform and report to me."

Having passed the BSM's inspection, it was a despondent Charlie who returned to the hut. Another chap and I feigned regret, but, as a token of sympathy, we blancoed his kit and cleaned his boots with spit and polish.

The other chap and I were stretched out on our beds the following morning when in burst Hewitt with full marching kit and rifle. "I'm not going," he called out, "The BSM says it's too late to send anybody now." We all burst out laughing, but Hewitt had the edge as it wasn't every gunner who had two batmen for an evening. Incidentally, we put our trousers under our mattresses to retain the creases. And, at Notton's, an outfitter in the town, I had my battledress blouse box pleated and the collar faced to be more presentable when wearing a tie.

LONDON DOCKS

I corresponded regularly with my brother, Ian, who was a radio officer/purser with Alfred Holt & Co. of Liverpool; owners of the Blue Funnel Line and the Glen Line. His ship, the "Glengarry", was on its way home from the Far East and he had told me to keep an eye on either the Journal of Commerce or Lloyd's Shipping Gazette to find out when she would dock in London so that we could meet. But, when the "Glengarry" arrived at King George V dock during the afternoon of 28 April, I was unable to be there because I was at Welbeck.

However, when Ian rejoined the ship on Monday, 23 May, I was able to spend that and subsequent evenings with him; until the "Glengarry" sailed again for the Far East on the 26th. And, when I left the ship just minutes before she cast off from the quay, Ian commented that I could have disembarked with the Thames' River Pilot at Gravesend.

A.A. PRACTICE CAMP, WEYBOURNE, NORFOLK

The Battery had returned from the Albert Hall rally and a mate of mine told me of a conversation he had had with a National Serviceman.

"What group are you?" he had asked.

The young soldier gave his number.

"Your lucky," said my lying mate, "mine is ....." and quoted a higher number.

"And," said my mate to me, "You have no idea how that bucked that chap's spirits up."

In order to practise firing real ammunition again, the regiment was moving to the AA Practice Camp at

Weybourne. Prior to leaving, I was bathhouse orderly, with Jack Jarvis as my assistant until he left for Weybourne with the Advance Party. L/Bdr Ken Ashley replaced Jack and, when, on 31 May, we learned that everyone was to be on a route march starting at 11am, we happily cleaned the baths and, to the chagrin of the other NCOs, managed to dodge the march.

As it was a lovely afternoon, the whole battery stopped dodging and played cricket. Sergeant 'Cannonball' Connor was in bat and, when I knocked the bails off when he was out of the crease, he wouldn't submit to the umpire's decision of 'out'. But when exactly the same thing happened on the very next ball, he was forced to retire.

This behaviour of Canonball was similar to that which he had shown during a football match the previous December when our troop was beaten by nine goals to one. On that occasion, he had nearly come to blows with Sgt. Titherington, a big and decent chap, who later said that, "If Cannonball's playing in future, count me out." (Later, at Weybourne Camp, Cannonball had a disagreement with another sergeant and received a black eye.)

Gunner Hartley, broke as usual, was trying to sell some possessions to raise capital. "How'd you like to buy this lanyard?"
"What would I be wanting wi' a lanyard?"
"Let's have a look at it. Why, you twerp, Hartley, it's mine."
"Pity," says Hartley. "7/6d (37½p) for a leather jacket then?" (I'm thinking it over. They're 30/- (£1.50) in the shops.)

"I'm pretty skint," says I, with £2.10/- (£2.50p) in my pocket, "Can't afford 5/- (35p) tonight." And, after some haggling, I eventually got the jacket for 1/6d (7½p).

I was writing a letter on the evening of 1 June when Cannonball, who had just returned from leave, entered our hut to tell us that an inspection was to be held at 9am the following morning.

"This is a fine time to tell us," I grumbled.

"What do you mean?" he asked.

"Well, my kit's all messy and I'll have to blanco it. Couldn't you have told us a week ago?"

"A week ago? You're in the Army now my lad. And get these windows cleaned too."

"Doing something more important, sarg."

"What?"

"Writing a letter home," I.replied.

Cannonball and I had become quite friendly and due more to his wife's insistence rather than his own inclination, he was leaving the Army in August. He divulged to me that he was somewhat anxious about what he was going to do in civvy street although he had done a six-month course in plumbing.

On the eve of our departure for Weybourne, Cannonball was in a foul mood. The state of the Barrack Room met with his disapproval and every little thing annoyed him.

"What are you doing?"

"Nothing, sarg."

"Well, parade with the guard tonight." And so it went on until he had most of my roommates on parade with the guard in full marching order.

When I was in the NCOs' bar at NAAFI break and saw him at the door searching the crowd for someone, I made to crawl under a table, but he spotted me. "You're on a charge. Your room's filthy."

"Couldn't I have my NAAFI break first?" I asked. But he wouldn't hear of it.

Later, when he had cooled down, he came and sat on my bed. "OK, you can go now," I said.

A surprised look appeared on his face. "What do you mean?" he asked.

"I've seen some fellows in a lousy mood, but yours beats everything. I'm really surprised at you." This hurt his feelings and he began humming and hawing in an apologetic manner. Cannonball, who was 38 and plenty tough, was really a great guy and I had a long talk with him on our special train to Weybourne the next day; Saturday, 4 June, 1949.

On arriving at Weybourne Railway Station, we adjusted our battle order before marching to the camp. As the Advance Party had pitched the tents, it didn't take long to settle in and I had no sooner made my bed and changed than I was out on patrol of the small village with Cannonball and another Lance Jack. Most of our *patrol*, however, was spent in a licensed café and, when it closed, we returned to the camp in a tillie; a small Army van.

There were four of us to a tent, sleeping on palliasses on wooden boarding, and, in the cramped conditions, it was difficult to sleep on the first night. My tent, the last in No.2 line, was only about 250 yards from the sea and, lying in the darkness, something like the following conversation ensued: "Did you see the cluster of beasties at the top of the pole?"

"The earwigs? Yes."

"They can crawl into your ear, you know."

"I know. I remember reading that in the News of the World, but they come out in the morning."

"Yes, but what if they lay their eggs there? They could hatch out and eat your brain."

"Only if you've got one. Let's go to sleep."

But some plugged their ears with paper - just in case.

The next morning, Sunday, we had a parade, lined off tents and laid out kit before lunchtime. After that, we were free and there was a sixpenny (2½p) dance in the camp cinema at night. Unfortunately, the band didn't show so that we danced to records, but as one hundred ATS girls were due in the following day, we considered that next Sunday's dance would be better anyway.

The target for our firing practice was a sleeve, pulled at a considerable distance behind a 'plane. On the first day, and after a few successful mock runs, we were ready for the real thing. The sequence, prior to the final instruction, was gone through and, in the Control Room, we stood ready for the order to fire. But, suddenly someone yelled STOP and we froze. The guns were aimed, not at the target, but at the 'plane.

Another time, we used what was known as a 180° throw-off when the 'plane, without a sleeve, flew behind us and we fired out to sea on a reciprocal bearing. When calculations were made, it was found that we had hit the target nine times out of 17 attempts.

(At Gravesend, we once travelled to a Light AA site where, inside a large dome-shaped building, a film was projected on the ceiling showing an enemy plane hedgehopping over a landscape. And, using a Light AA gun, possibly a Bofors, we had to bring down the plane. No calculations were necessary, but you had to be quick as it was only a matter of seconds between the plane's appearance and its passing over your head.)

On my return to the tent after tea, my comrades told me, with great enthusiasm, that a NAAFI girl wanted a date with me and that they had arranged that I meet her outside the NAAFI at 2000 hours. Although deducing this to be a practical joke, I said nothing, but dressed in my best uniform and their injunctions to have a good time followed me as I left the tent - heading, not for the NAAFI, but for Sheringham.

As I had suspected, there was no date and the jokers had waited outside the NAAFI to witness, and enjoy, my disappointment. But, as the girl had not been on duty that night and I said that we had had a good time, they didn't know what to make of it.

For some reason, Jack Jarvis had retired from the hairdressing business so that I was the sole barber at Weybourne. At 6d (2½p) a time, I made 12/- (60p) cash down, plus a few on the book for collection on payday, on one Sunday alone. This was because I had a monopoly, as, unlike Gravesend, there was no competition from local barbers. In fact, I believe I scalped about an eighth of the battery as so many men approached me after they had been given the order "Get your hair cut" when on parade.

A gunner, previously a London barrow boy, was the most fussy. "Have you cut hair before?" he asked. "Yes," I replied, but, not trusting me, he produced his own mirror so that, using it in conjunction with mine, he could see every clip I made at the back of his head. During my time as a barber, only one customer reneged on payment, but as that was the notorious Brady, I didn't feel it prudent to pursue the matter.

One Saturday evening, a group of us had a very pleasant and amusing time in an old inn in Sherringham. The inn was busy with some playing dominos and others playing Devil Among The Tailors or Bar Skittles – a game where nine pins, standing on a square table, are knocked down by a ball, attached to a string and swung round a pole.

When we sat down at a table, one of the chaps said, "What about a game of blind dominos?"

"What's that?" we asked.

"Well, instead of playing the easy way, you must lay the dominos upside down so that you're opponent can't see what they are. At the end of the game turn them over and they all work out OK."

"Ridiculous", "Impossible" and "Nuts" were our comments.

"Come here, Eric." said the gunner and pulled me aside.

We returned to the table and began playing. The old men became interested and leaned over our shoulders. They were baffled. "Oh, anybody can play the usual way," we said, "but here you have to use your brains." We never laid down a piece without first staring fixedly into each other's eyes and when a local asked how it was done, we said, "Telepathy." When the dominos were turned over at the end of the game and were seen to be perfectly linked, a cheer went up. But we didn't divulge the secret. It wasn't our eyes that needed watching, but our feet! With my right foot on his left and his feet likewise positioned, we had tapped out the numbers required.

MUTINY

When some members of my squad, who had been on guard duty only two nights previously, learned that they were due to be on again that night, they complained to me that it was unfair. "They're making use of us, just because we're getting near demob," they moaned. (The guard was composed of five men, only three of whom did duty at the gate; doing two hours on and four hours off. Neither the Guard Commander nor the 'Stickman', deemed to be the best turned-out and who, I seem to remember, ran errands for the others, did gate duty.)

"Let's do this properly," I said, "FALL IN." We marched smartly to the offices and I gave the orders, 'HALT. STAND EASY', before going in. I had expected the BSM to be alone, but a 2nd lieutenant who, I believe, was a professional footballer, stood beside him. "I've come to report a complaint, sir," I began and stated the men's complaint.

The RSM was angry and, glancing through his window at the men outside, he replied, "This constitutes mutiny, Bombardier."
"No, sir," I said, "I'm representing the men." At this point, the lieutenant asked me to leave and I marched the men back to the tents.

An hour or so later, new orders were placed on the notice board and the guard whooped with joy as they made way for me to read them. With one exception, the guard had been changed, but this was fair enough as I hadn't been Guard Commander on the previous occasion.

Hickie told me to do a job on the tracker at 7.30am, after I'd switched it on at 6am in preparation for action. "I'm not familiar with it, sir," I prevaricated.

Jack Smith, a regular, then piped up - "I know how to do it, sir,"

"OK," says Hickie, "You do it then and (to me) you can go along with him."

Some time later, when I realized it was better to be beside the tracker in the open air than in the stuffy Control Room, Hickie asked, "Have you finished these checks?"

"Not yet," I replied, "It's only the second time or so that I've done them and I must follow the instruction book."

"No time for learning," says Hickie, "Bombardier Smith knows how it's done."

"Suit yourself," I said, "but I know, myself, now."

The 'suit yourself' riled Hickie, but he allowed me to finish the job."

With our demob only a matter of weeks away, we were all 'demob happy'. "What are you looking so happy about, Bombardier?" asked Hickie the next day.

"Two weeks, two days, sir," I replied.

"Don't be too sure," says he.

When medical examinations were conducted a few days before we left Weybourne, I was passed as Grade A1, and during our last night, we slept on bare boards as we had been ordered to burn our palliasses.

DEMOB

Monday 27 June was to be the *Great Day* and, on our return to Gravesend on Saturday, the occupants of our hut could talk about little else than demob. Demob was an obsession and we heard that one group had trashed a barrack room and had to pay for the damage.

For us, however, it was low-key. We exchanged addresses and promised to write, although few ever did. Major Auret said goodbye to us and, when he shook my hand, he said, "I hardly know what to say to you. I think you're a grand fellow." And, with nothing but demob on my mind, Sunday seemed a long day and I mooned about feeling absolutely lost.

Together with the others in Group 111, I travelled by train to Aldershot on Monday. At the Demobilization Centre, we handed in our kit, were given £5, told to 'Git out of it' and, wearing our civilian clothes, we joyfully did so. That was it. It was all over. And, exactly two week later, I was back at my desk in the Dundee office.

Printed in Great Britain
by Amazon